ANANDA

Where Yoga Lives

John Ball

Bowling Green University Popular Press
Bowling Green, Ohio 43403

Library of Congress Catalog Card No.: 82-082100

ISBN: 0-87972-207-X Clothbound
        0-87972-208-8 Paperback

Cover concept by John Ball
Artwork by Alice Thompson

Dedication

For H.R.F. Keating
brilliant colleague and cherished friend
whose wish was gratified

CONTENTS

Swami Kriyananda

Foreword

For some time we here at Ananda have been aware that we had an extraordinary story to tell. When we first started our community in 1968, with high hopes but very little else, the odds against our success were astronomical. We knew it, but we decided to try anyway.

After ten years, a devastating forest fire, and some near miraculous recoveries from mishaps and looming disasters, we were not only still here, we were meeting with a success we had not dared to believe could ever be ours.

From the very first I had been convinced that we were under the protection and guidance of our guru, Paramhansa Yogananda. I suspect that the Pilgrims felt the same way, that they were under a very special benevolence, on the *Mayflower*.

We set out to found a spiritual community dedicated to the teachings of the man with whom I spent many precious years of my life. He told me that he had a job for me to do, and he also many times reiterated that he wanted to see a group of communities dedicated to the high ideals and practices of yoga; and to the brotherhood of man. When the time came, I did my best to follow his directive.

God must be pleased with us, He has done so much on our behalf. Where, quite literally, many thousands of communities have failed, ours has succeeded. It has reached the point where we are going through the legal process of incorporating as a town:—Ananda, California. We have much about which to be grateful.

Ever since our tenth anniversary, I have been hoping to find someone to tell the story: not for our own aggrandizement, but to share our inspiration with others and, hopefully, to reach the many thousands who might like to know more about our unique way of life. Although there are several hundred of us

1

here at Ananda proper and in our several satellite centers, there was no one who seemed to be the right person to put the truly remarkable Ananda story on paper. Obviously for me to attempt it myself would be in dubious taste, as would be engaging someone to write about us for a fee.

My real hope was somehow to find an author of established stature who might be persuaded to consider us a worthy subject. Then through a chain of unusual circumstances, John Ball came to Ananda. He had no personal desire to visit us, but he had a close friend from England who had asked to see an American ashram. Mr. Ball had found our name in a directory and when he called us, we assured him that we would be most happy to welcome him and his party. He became our friend and when enough time had passed, I ventured to suggest to him that he write about Ananda. Our guru saw to it that he accepted.

Mr. Ball is, of course, the internationally-known author of *In the Heat of the Night* and many other books that are currently published in many languages. To help persuade him, I offered to open our files to him *in toto*, and to provide him with any and all information that he might require. Despite the fact that he is primarily a novelist, and a highly successful one, he did undertake the project and devoted many months of his time to a penetrating research of our background and activities.

This is our story as he has consented to tell it. Allow me to add that if you find this account as fascinating as I believe it to be, you are most welcome to come and visit us also, if you so desire.

> S. Kriyananda
>
> Ananda Cooperative Village
> Nevada City, California

"I have a great work for you to do."

Paramhansa Yogananda to Donald Walters

"For thirty years I had envisioned a community and had studied ways that might make it possible, but I was very anxious that it be God's will. I was a lone disciple of Master, not in the mainstream of his work any more, but desperately wanting to serve him in some way. That is why I was reluctant: I didn't want to do something that might be wrong. I wanted to be awfully sure I was being guided. When the time at last came, God forced it down my throat."

Swami Kriyananda

Preface

Whenever the subject of communities and communal living comes up, a variety of doubts and suspicions is usually aroused. The possible brainwashing of impressionable young people is frequently mentioned. Although the idea itself is centuries old, it has yet to be accepted as an approved method of living, even in this so-called New Age.

Community dwellers are currently often regarded as either religious crackpots or drug abusing freaks who may or may not be living under "free love" conditions. When the theory of group marriage was promulgated, it followed automatically that communal living would have to be a part of its structure. The belief that a community is essentially a collection of drop-outs is common. And now, inevitably, over the whole idea of community living there hangs the horror of Jonestown.

Of many hundreds that have been started, very few have proven successful. Findhorn, in northern Scotland, was the subject of a popular book that appeared in 1975. This colony attracted considerable notice because, in a near impossible climate and out of virtually hopeless soil, the residents created a garden so lush and productive as to be regarded by many as supernatural. According to the book, *The Magic of Findhorn,* the earth spirits are in steady communication with the community and it is through their guidance that such phenomenal results have been achieved.

The Ananda community in northern California makes no claims of direct assistance from such extraordinary beings, but its history is nevertheless remarkable. It is a spiritual colony headed by a fully accredited swami who is an American with an international reputation in his field through his teachings and writings.

The fact that Ananda has done so remarkably well against terrifying odds, and that at every time of crisis help always seems to come in some extraordinary way, invites attention. So also does the fact that in thirteen years, despite many mishaps and several potentially fatal accidents, no one has ever been seriously injured.

At one time the community was facing a series of pressing bills totaling many thousands of dollars with no resources to meet more than a few of them. The last week before the payment deadline a totally unexpected donation of considerable size was received. When all of the outstanding obligations had been satisfied in full, and imminent disaster had been averted, precisely $1.37 was left in the treasury.

An Ananda truck coming down a steep, winding mountain road completely lost its brakes and crashed through a thin guard rail over an almost sheer 1000 foot drop. It was caught and held by a solitary tree that was growing in the one and only spot where it could prevent a certain fatal plunge. No one was even slightly injured.

When a young woman fell twelve feet off a construction platform and was impaled on a huge 12 inch spike, she felt no pain at all. The doctor who gave her emergency treatment reported that the spike had somehow, by a hair's breadth, missed every vein, artery, and vital area of her body. Furthermore, he stated, no surgeon could have made a more exact incision. She was up and about again, fully recovered, in two weeks.

Many great yogis have reportedly appeared to selected disciples after their *mahasamadhis,* or earthly deaths. If Paramhansa Yogananda chooses to appear at Ananda, he will find himself very much at home. All of the residents are his dedicated disciples although none of them, except their leader, knew him in life. They revere him because through him they feel very close to God.

During his lifetime, which ended in 1952, Yogananda called for the founding of spiritual communities dedicated to world brotherhood and to "simple living and high thinking." Ananda is the first response to this directive. Its remarkable history, and its present expanding horizons, are the subject of this work.

Chapter One

The Realm of Joy

Nevada County, which lies in Northern California east and a little north of Sacramento, is rich in both history and spectacular scenery. A century ago it was a focal point in the rush for gold and in some areas the devastation wrought by hydraulic mining is still stark and awesome. More happily, it also includes part of the majestic western slope of the Sierras where one magnificent panorama can be found on top of another. From an altitude close to sea level the county rises to eight thousand feet. More than half of its total area is given over to national forests where vast stands of timber cover the rolling hills and lower mountains.

Because of its location and the nature of its terrain, it is a natural breeding ground for wild life. In particular, the eastern half abounds with deer.

When the heat of August begins to subside, and September takes over with its beginning of fall colors on the countless thousands of leaf-bearing trees, the time of the hunting season draws closer. Archers are legally permitted to bag game from August 23rd to September 14th, but they are not quite as deadly as are the men with the guns. From the time the shooting season opens on September 20th until it closes on November 2nd, down many of the rural or wooded roads a hunter will be stationed almost every fifty feet, poised and ready to make a kill.

But before the guns are taken down, oiled and loaded, an unexplained phenomenon begins to take place in a region located a few miles north of Nevada City on the opposite side of the South Yuba River. For many miles around, the deer begin to show signs of restlessness as mid-September approaches.

Then, five or six days before the shooting season officially begins, they start a gradual migration. By some knowledge or instinct that no naturalist has as yet been able to define, they gradually converge on a piece of farmland that lies on Tyler Foote Rood a few miles from its junction with Highway 49.

There is nothing about the 600-plus acres of the farm that would particularly strike an observer as unusual apart from the presence of some buildings scattered about and a few roads cut through the property. But the deer know. They come to the farm quietly, munching bits of grass as they make their way, guided, some believe, by the very vibrations in the soil. When they finally arrive they often lie quietly down and wait, unhurried and contented. For they are safe; the property they are on is protected. It is not only a place where no hunting is permitted; it is a place where they are welcome, where the many human beings about will not harm them, and where the children will often pet their gentle heads and soft flanks. It is a place called Ananda.

Ananda is a Sanskrit word which means *joy*. The translation is not exact; the original meaning implies permanence rather than just a momentary surge of delight or happiness. It also suggests a deep-seated spiritual emotion so solidly entrenched that no ordinary setback, or even disaster, can cause it to be destroyed.

The place called Ananda is a community made up of men, women and children who represent a wide age span and many different religious upbringings. Some eleven percent of the Ananda membership is of Jewish origin. There are also Roman Catholics, Protestants of varying denominations, and some persons who have never previously professed any specific form of worship. In the environment of Ananda, it makes no difference. The residents came to the community for a variety of different personal reasons. What makes them so distinctive, if not unique, is the extraordinary success they have achieved.

Almost as soon as the first settlers arrived from Europe onto the shores of the New World, the already old idea of having communities of "like minded souls" was once again seriously considered. Often what was visualized was a commune where all property would be shared and all individual aspirations would be pooled for the common good. Through the passing years of the nation's history literally hundreds of communities and communes, designed according to varying formats, have come into being. A few prospered for a time, often because of the leadership of a particularly charismatic individual, but the great majority floundered and most sank within a month's time.

In the opinion of many people, the whole community idea is foredoomed by the structure of human nature. It is not realistic, they argue, to expect to assemble any considerable number of laymen and women who will be virtually free from such common attributes as personal ambition, pride of possession, or the simple desire for status and recognition. People who will consistently love their fellow men and women as well as themselves, they hold, will always be in short supply.

But despite all the visible objections, the community idea has continued to survive and has been tried out time and again. Almost always initial hopes were high, but they were seldom matched by achieved realities. Then, beginning in 1967, came Ananda.

Physically the community, like Caesar's Gaul, is divided into three parts. The main section, which lies almost entirely north of Tyler Foote Road, is known simply as The Farm. It is 611 acres of gently sloped farmland and wooded areas that rises from 2500 feet to almost 3000 feet in altitude. At this location the air is clear and the climate is mild. It can grow somewhat cool in winter, but when snow does fall it is usually very light and normally disappears in a matter of hours.

At the southeast corner of The Farm is the present Reception Center and Apprentice Village. Here an old farmhouse and garage have been converted to new uses. There is also a scattering of additional outbuildings, some of which serve as residences.

A short distance farther down Tyler Foote Road, where the Ananda property does not quite reach the highway, an easement road leads into what is called "Downtown Ananda." There is a road junction here and a guardpost that is manned at night. Close by is the grocery and general store that is known as Master's Market. Also in the immediate area are some of the community offices, a shower and sanitation building, a girl's ashram, and a very old barn that manages to house some of the privately owned Ananda cottage industries. Five minute's walk up a gentle hill is the impressive publications building which holds many additional offices.

Just north of The Farm, and separated from it by scarcely 300 feet, is an eighteen and a half acre parcel of wooded land that has been named *Ayodhya*. Here, in semi-isolation, is the monastery area where the renunciate monks of the community live. Also on this property is the home of Swami Kriyananda. It is principally a geodesic dome thirty-six feet in diameter with a small recording studio and an impressive office attached.

Some six driving miles east and south of the The Farm, and available only by means of a fire access road, is the Ananda Meditation Retreat. This is the original property where the community, or more properly, cooperative village, first took root. The 67 acres of the Retreat house some of the permanent residents, in particular those who have a special wish for seclusion or who prefer to live very simply in the woods.

At the Retreat there is a small complex of buildings which includes the temple, the Common Dome and a kitchen area. There are also some limited accommodations for guests. Many more would be desirable, for each year hundreds of visitors come to the Retreat to participate in the classes given there in the yoga postures, meditation, philosophy and practical spiritual living. The retreatants are given the opportunity of meeting many of the Ananda resident members and sharing in the community life.

Although the title to this piece of land is clear, it is held in conjunction with three other parcels by a group of four known as the Bald Mountain Association. By agreement with the other property owners, Ananda has restricted any further construction or development at the Retreat so that the immediate area may be kept a largely undisturbed haven for the benefit of those who prefer it that way.

Since the Sunday services were held at the Retreat temple for many years, the residents of The Farm had to travel a considerable distance to attend. Many walked the twelve mile round trip when enough transportation was not available. By the mid 1970s it had become apparent that the temple was no longer adequate. And since the continuing growth of the community was not only steady, but also accelerating, obviously something needed to be done.

In 1979 construction began on a long-planned World Brotherhood Center and new temple at The Farm. When the still uncompleted temple was first used in the summer of 1980, an estimated 400 worshipers were present at the initial service. As the planners surveyed the congregation on that significant occasion, the disquieting thought must have struck them that once again they had seriously underestimated. Since the total population of Ananda had doubled within the preceding year, they went back to their drawing boards in some haste. There they undertook the design of a still larger and more magnificent temple, but like those who were laying out commercial airports in the 1930s, they could not be sure how rapidly growth factors might make their careful work obsolete even before it could be completed.

The land at The Farm and at *Ayodhya* is all held by the Yoga Fellowship, a non-profit religious corporation. This is necessary to avoid having the community classed as a subdivision, a step which would impose a large number of requirements and restrictions. As a consequence Ananda residents do not hold title to either their homes or the land on which they stand. The whole property also falls under the Nevada County Zoning Ordinance which permits only one dwelling unit per five acres.

In 1973 Ananda complied with a legal requirement that it submit a master plan for its future development to the Nevada County Planning Commission. The work was undertaken internally since Ananda included an experienced city planner among its residents. The community was told that approximately six months would be required for final approval of the plan; while such approval was pending a moratorium on all new construction was imposed.

Possibly because the county authorities had never had to deal with anything approaching a similar situation, the process took far longer than expected. Innumerable technicalities were raised to the point where three separate plans had to be developed. Before approval was finally granted, a full five years had passed. During all this time the building moratorium remained in effect. As a result an acute housing shortage arose. It was greatly intensified when twenty one of the Ananda homes were destroyed by fire. Nevertheless somehow the community managed to cope. When, as a last straw, a huge tree fell onto a small home and completely destroyed it, the Ananda residents accepted the fact that God was simply being thorough.

During the first service in the new temple, in July 1980, the mortgage on the original farm property was burned, relieving the community of a $2,000 monthly payment that it had been meeting for more than a decade. But the visible real estate holdings, and the various improvements that have been made, do not in themselves constitute more than a stage on which the continuing drama of Ananda is being enacted.

The unifying element throughout the community, and the inspiration for its existence, is the teachings of the late Indian yoga master Paramhansa Yogananda. He was, according to his followers, an *avatar*, a fully liberated person of great spiritual attainment who was, quite literally, one of God's representatives here on earth. Not the only one by any means, but a divinely inspired individual who was sent from India to bring a greater and deeper awareness of God to the western world. It is a matter of record that during his lifetime he succeeded to a remarkable degree.

Yogananda utilized many avenues in the furtherance of his work, but one that he cherished was not to be successfully realized during his lifetime. In his own words, "To spread a spirit of brotherhood among all peoples and to aid in establishing, in many countries, self-sustaining world-brotherhood colonies for plain living and high thinking." The church that he established in 1920, the Self Realization Fellowship, was not to carry this objective forward, but from its ranks came the man who did. He is an American now internationally known by his earned title of Swami Kriyananda. He is the founder of Ananda and is its spiritual leader.

Ananda was established to make Yogananda's dream a reality, and to an impressive degree it is doing so. The people who make up its membership all share a dedication to him and to the yogic philosophy that he taught. It is doubtful if there is a room of any kind at Ananda, public or private, that does not display a picture of him. He is commonly referred to as "Master" and even the grocery store is named in his honor.

It is at Ananda that the savants are confounded; where not only the improbable, but also the near impossible, has come to pass. Some of the residents have been there for less than a year, but there are a great many who have lived in the community for five years, ten years, and more. Some are still quite young, others are entitled to senior citizen status. They have come from all parts of the United States, from Canada and from abroad. They represent many different ethnic origins and widely varying economic backgrounds, but through their efforts and combined will they have become members of a closely integrated family. This unity is firm and everywhere visible; even a first time visitor cannot escape sensing the solidarity of the community, one which closely resembles an actual blood relationship.

It is not a facade, like the shaking of hands outside a church by people who barely know each other, because the service just concluded has made it the thing to do. The commitment at Ananda is of a totally different kind. It is found everywhere, from the apprentice village to the men and women who have gladly taken vows of renunciation and who look forward to a lifetime of dedication to God, to guru (Yogananda), and to the service of humanity.

At one time Swami Kriyananda was moved to remark, "Utopian communities are food for dreams, but almost never for action." At the time he was probably thinking of an idealized environment where absolute perfection would continuously prevail. Ananda has never laid claim to that. In fact, at one point, to quote the swami again, he was "perhaps beginning to sense the absurdity of trying to perfect anything so inherently unstable as human society."

Perfection is almost by definition unattainable, but the motivating spirit and dedication of the people of Ananda have accomplished more than all but a few would have thought possible a little more than a decade ago. The key to this achievement, in Ananda's own terms, is personal transformation.

The children who attend the Ananda schools learn something more than the conventional academic subjects (on which they test out, on a statewide basis, at one or two full grades above the norm). At one time an Ananda mother, sorely pressed by other matters, was unduly annoyed when her seven year old son misbehaved and upbraided him severely. Shortly thereafter, realizing that she had gone too far, she called her little son to her and apologized. "That's all right, mother," he told her, "I knew that God was only testing you through me."

It is reasonable to assume that those who come to enter the Apprentice Village, or who enroll in the courses given at the Mediterranean Retreat, are at least somewhat preconditioned toward accepting new patterns of thought and conduct. A case in point is a community resident who, when asked what had first attracted him to Ananda, replied, "Excitement at the idea that there *was a place* where people really cared about the well-being of others, and high principles were practiced in each moment of life."

The community has arranged things so that people may come for a week end, a whole week, a month, several months, or a lifetime. Visitors will find classes and instruction in many things, from the highly spiritual to the very practical; from Kriya Yoga to organic gardening and animal husbandry. They may take part in an active social and spiritual program, or they can enjoy almost total seclusion if that is what they prefer. For the various Retreat programs there are different schedules of fees; each retreatant may choose which one he wishes to pay, according to his own means.

Ananda is a cooperative village within which each resident has his or her own personal property and, quite possibly, business enterprise. It is not a commune where all material goods are pooled for the common welfare. Individual privacy is fully respected and even though the residents at present do not hold title to their homes; if they built or paid for them and then should wish to move for any reason, they are repaid for their investment.

Life at Ananda is in no way posh. Few of the houses have the convenience of an indoor toilet. Some are of minimal size, little larger than a good two-car garage. Many people live in trailers. But within every square yard of the grounds there is a deeply imbedded sense and feeling of spiritual joy. The lack of amenities does not seem to matter at all. Most of the members of the community are vegetarians and together they grow approximately half of their own food. The Ananda dairy supplies milk products and related items.

Unemployment among the residents is normally nil. Most of the members work in one of the community's activities and draw salaries. The pay scales are modest, but so is the cost of residing on the grounds. Among the residents are two medical doctors, several attorneys, and many other professional people. There are also skilled workers who represent a wide range of competence.

But when the land, the buildings and the people are all combined, they still do not add up to the sum total that is Ananda. For there is a very powerful added factor: the spirituality that pervades the whole community. It permeates everything: the classrooms, the offices, the open fields and the gardens, and along every pathway.

It is invisible, but it can be felt. When the bulk of each day is over, and the final hour before sleep comes, the people of Ananda sit silently, their hands laid, palms up, at the point where the legs meet the torso. Their eyes are closed and silence surrounds them. They are in meditation, their minds turned toward God, communing with Him, letting comfort and peace fill their beings. And when they pray they pray for everyone. In the richness of their meditation mundane cares and worries are lifted away, a sense of nearness to eternity grows stronger, and a kind of cosmic vibration seems to enter the soul.

There was a girl who came to Ananda. Although she was still young, her life had been turbulent and she had once even attempted suicide. She came as many others have come, wondering if by any chance this place of which she had heard might somehow hold something that would give meaning to her life.

She drove slowly onto the grounds, stopped and got out. She looked about her and then walked a few steps away from the ancient vehicle that had managed to get her there. She stood very still and took several deep breaths. Then something came over her. It was as real as the sky overhead and the air she was breathing. She saw the fields, the wooded areas, the few simple buildings that served as the heart of the community. Then, very quietly, she said to herself, "I'm home."

Chapter Two

Missionary to the West

Early in the morning of 19 September 1920 an ocean-going vessel called *The City of Sparta* nosed her way into Pier 3 of Chelsea Harbor, part of the port of Boston, Massachusetts. She was two months out of India, the first of her kind to make that voyage since World War I. On the passenger list, according to his passport, was a 27 year old native of Bengal, one Makunda Lal Ghosh. He was clad in an ochre robe which emphasized his somewhat chunky figure. He also had on a turban, not one of the firm tight variety usually worn by Sikhs, but a loose-appearing one that seemed about to fall off at any moment. As he stepped for the first time onto the soil of the New World his heart and mind were full of the work he was to do: he was a missionary come from India to bring a better understanding of God to America.

He had been invited to come as the delegate from India to an International Congress of Religious Liberals in America. After that he would be on his own, a fact that did not disconcert him. He had been assured by his guru that the time had come for the eyes of the West to be opened; the task of bringing that about had been given to him.

His arrival was not noted by the fundamentalist preachers of the Bible Belt. Had they known of him, they would undoubtedly have blasted invective against the man who had come to teach the ancient science of yoga and the spiritual blessings of meditation. And had they known also that he was prepared to explain the nature of karma, and the doctrine of reincarnation, there would probably have been some alarming heart seizures amongst them. It is therefore perhaps just as well that this unique visitor from India arrived rather quietly.

17

The press, however, did not miss him. As the delegates to the forthcoming Congress gathered, a photographer sent to cover the story spotted the colorful Indian at once. With sure instinct he put him in the front row center of the picture he was about to take. The rest of the delegates in the photograph were all dignified gentlemen in formal attire, religious liberals by definition, but certainly not in appearance. The man from India was certainly, a standout.

Despite his relative youth, he was a swami, a fully initiated member of that ancient order. He had been received into it in 1914 at the age of twenty one, shortly after his graduation from college. On a sunny Thursday afternoon in July Swami Sri Yukteswar had dipped a piece of white cloth in ochre dye and when it had dried had draped it across the shoulders of his young disciple, a symbolic renunciate's robe. Foregoing much of the usual ritual, which was not to his taste, Yukteswar invited the initiate to choose his own monastic name. After only a moment's thought, Mukunda made his decision. "Yogananda," he said. It was a fairly common name which many before him had also selected. It translates "bliss [ananda] through divine union [yoga]." From that moment forward he was Swami Yogananda, his birth name permanently abandoned. With total conviction and without reservation, he dedicated his life to God.

When, six years later, he set out to take up his life's work in the United States, he had prepared himself by learning English. He was not, however, very confident of his abilities in that language. During the long voyage to the New World he was invited to speak to the other passengers on the topic "The Battle of Life and How to Fight It." It was to be the first time that he would attempt to speak in public in English and the thought terrified him. He tried to prepare himself and failed. When he was introduced he stood up and at once encountered a complete case of stage fright.

He could not retreat, he could not sit down, and he was vocally paralyzed. For ten long, agonizing minutes he stood there in silence. Fortunately the audience understood his predicament and there was some gentle laughter. In desperation he appealed to his guru, undoubtedly in Bengali. Back came a thundering answer. "You *can*! Speak!" The inhibitions that had frozen him vanished; forty five minutes later his audience was still intently listening.

On October 6, in what was described in the press as "fluent English," Yogananda addressed the Congress; his topic was "The Science of Religion." He was well received; his mission had begun.

He remained in Boston for the following three years, teaching those who came to him the basic techniques of yoga and of meditation; to some he revealed the secret of the Kriya. As his reputation grew, so did his following. In November 1923 he successfully invaded New York. A little more than six months later he departed on a major transcontinental tour that took him to most of the nation's major cities. He began to fill large auditoriums. Viewed dispassionately, his success considerably exceeded what might have been expected, particularly since he was not offering a popular new fad or a claimed startling revelation, but instead was teaching one of the oldest religious sciences known.

Most American worship, regardless of denomination, has for many generations been wrapped in dogma. The same rituals have been repeated endlessly, inevitably introducing an element of boredom capable of penetrating even very sincere and devout minds. Yogananda asked no one to abandon his or her basic beliefs, but he offered to all a ritual-free type of service that consisted of the singing of a few simple hymns he preferred to call chants, brief periods of meditation, and messages that were largely atuned to everyday living.

On one occasion he kept an audience in Carnegie Hall enthusiastically singing *Oh God Beautiful* for an hour and a half. He had a remarkable personal magnetism and despite his youth, no one questioned his deep knowledge of the yogic philosophy. Many, of course, disapproved of him, but that did not seem to bother him at all. He knew where he was going because he felt that God was guiding his way.

For some time he continued to address public gatherings, often with hundreds turned away. When the great depression came and devastated the lives of tens of thousands of people, perhaps his message of a different and very direct path to the Creator gave the hope that so many desperate people needed. Whatever the reason, the swami from India found an acceptance, and often an enthusiasm, that no one familiar with the nation's relatively fixed religious practices and beliefs could conceivably have forecast. To give it its rightful name, it was a phenomenon.

In 1935 he returned to India for a visit. There he was reunited with his guru who was already fully aware of his disciple's remarkable success in the New World. He had, in fact, anticipated it, because he had been told by a source so high it could not be questioned (Babaji—see later) that Yogananda would exceed all expectations

Without great ceremony, which he still disliked, Yukteswar gave Yogananda a few words of blessing and then conferred on him the title of Paramhansa, which superseded his former designation as swami. The new title literally translates as "highest swan," a reference to the fact that a swan, in Indian mythology, is, among other things, the means of transport of Brahma the Creator. Perhaps Wagner knew this when he created Lohengrin.*

When he returned to California Yogananda found that one of his foremost disciples, Mr. James Lynn, had built him a fine new retreat at Encinitas directly on the ocean. There the now fully accepted Master settled down and in his study, which has a commanding view of the seemingly endless Pacific, he wrote the book that has become a true spiritual classic, *The Autobiography of a Yogi.* The church that he had founded not long after his arrival in 1920, the Self Realization Fellowship,

---

*The correct spelling of Yogananda's new title has been the subject of some controversy. It has been rendered as both Paramhansa and Paramahansa. In the early editions of his book *The Autobiography of a Yogi* his portrait appears above a facsimile of his signature which reads *Paramhansa*. In later editions, released after his death, the signature has been cleverly but visibly doctored to read *Paramahansa*. The text also is considered revised in the later editions, something for which the Self Realization Fellowship, the publishers, have not chosen to give an explanation.

was firmly established and carrying on its work in many different countries.

He no longer desired to travel and address large crowds; rather he preferred to remain close to the Los Angeles area: at Encinitas, at the Mount Washington headquarters of the Self Realization Fellowship, and at a private retreat at Twenty Nine Palms. There he was able to work more closely with a selected group of his most promising disciples. In one important respect he was disappointed: he very much wanted to start a spiritual community of yoga devotees and he laid out careful plans for its organization.

The full story of Paramhansa Yogananda is found in the *Autobiography* and in other books by and about him. Of particular interest is *Man's Eternal Quest*, an anthology of his public addresses and talks taken down in shorthand by his dedicated disciple, Sri Daya Mata, and transcribed by her as a labor of love. A great deal about Yogananda is in *The Path: Autobiography of a Western Yogi* by Swami Kriyananda. Less well known, but deserving of attention, is *The Flawless Mirror* by Kamala, another of his very devoted disciples. (This work is somewhat difficult to locate; copies can be obtained from Ananda at $15.00.)

It was the life and teachings of Paramhansa Yogananda that caused the Ananda Cooperative Village to come into being. He is the guiding guru for everyone there, despite the fact that apart from Kriyananda none of them actually knew him or even heard him speak. He will never be superseded because, by his own statement, he was the last of a series of six gurus, or teachers, who collectively are the foundation stones on which Ananda, and the Self Realization Fellowship, are established.

It may surprise some that the first and greatest of these is Jesus Christ. He is profoundly venerated at Ananda and throughout the SRF. A life size statue of Him is the most prominent feature in the Ananda temple. Christmas is a very important event at the community while the SRF celebrates it with special services, open house at the Mother Center on Mount Washington, and a Christmas satsang (religious meeting) traditionally presided over by the president, since 1955 the greatly respected Sri Daya Mata. She is one of the first women ever to be admitted into the swami order.

The yogis look upon Christ as a great and divine teacher who was fully initiated into all the secrets of that ancient art. He is the supreme guide and guru and His presence is constantly sought in prayer and meditation.

The second in the series is Bhagavan (Lord) Krishna, a Hindu deity who was also reportedly an historical personage circa 3100 B.C. He is an incarnation of Vishnu the Preserver, the second in the Hindu trinity of Brahma, Vishnu and Shiva. He is most often depicted playing the flute, calling home true souls who have become entrapped in delusion. In Indian art he is shown as having a blue or blue/black skin. He was an *avatar*, or divine incarnation in human form.

As might be expected, no actual likeness of Krishna is known to exist. The portrait commonly used by Ananda and the SRF is not a fortunate choice; to a modern eye it appears to depict a woman rather than a man, but it is venerated none the less.

The third of the gurus is Babaji, and here the western mind may again encounter problems. They are, however, capable of resolution. Babaji is a living saint, so enormously advanced spiritually that he has extraordinary powers granted by God. These include a complete conquest over death. The name Babaji means "revered father"; his birth date, birth place and actual age are all presently unknown. Reputedly he has lived for centuries in the Himalayas surrounded by a very few close disciples who are obviously in a most privileged position.

Babaji appears as a young man with long, copper-colored hair. He is a *mahavatar*, or great avatar, who for a long period of history held the secret of Kriya Yoga until he revealed it to his disciple, Lahiri Mahasaya.

It is relatively easy to dismiss Babaji as a mythological being except for the fact that he has frequently appeared to persons of unquestioned integrity. These include not only his disciple, Lahira Mahasaya, but also Swami Sri Yukteswar, Paramhamsa Yogananda, and the saintly Sri Daya Mata.

Much about him will be found in *Autobiography of a Yogi*. It was Babaji who chose Yogananda to carry Kriya Yoga to the west. He so informed Yogananda's guru Sri Yukteswar, and sent Yogananda to him for training. Later he personally instructed Yogananda concerning his mission in a face-to-face meeting.

For the benefit of possible sceptics, Yogananda explained that some great spiritual beings, such as Christ, come to earth for a specific purpose and then depart. Others, such as Babaji, and many who are unknown, undertake work that will occupy them literally for centuries, covering the slow evolution of man rather than any single great purpose.

The most common picture of Babaji is a sketch made by an artist from a close description given him by Yogananda. It depicts a quite young man with his eyes cast heavenward. A much more compelling portrait, revealing the same features, has been painted by Sundaram, a distinguished fine artist who is a long-time Ananda resident.

The remaining three gurus are all recent historical personages about whom the facts are known and definite. The first of these is Lahiri Mhasaya (1828-1895). He is particularly esteemed because he was not a renunciate, but a married man, the father of two sons, and for thirty five years a faithful employee of the Indian government. Despite these worldly attachments he was a *Yogatavar*, or "incarnation of yoga." His guru was Babaji himself, who, as a supreme gift, taught him the technique of Kriya Yoga and instructed him to pass it on to those who were worthy to receive it. This Lahira did without regard to the religious beliefs of those he chose for the initiation.

The life of Lahiri Mahasaya is well documented, including many reported miracles that he performed. Despite his great fame and exalted spiritual status, he was a gentle and humble man who showed great respect for others and who asked very little for himself. The best known photograph of him shows him with his eyes half closed; it is one of the few pictures he permitted to be taken.

Lahiri's lasting gift to those who would follow in the path

of yoga was his demonstration that it was not necessary to become a monk or otherwise to renounce the world in order to achieve the greatest status as a guru. He held a modest job through most of his adult life, earning his living as countless other millions before and after him have had to do. He was a devoted family man, a householder, and at the same time a spiritual guide and teacher of the highest order. Many modern day initiates, when in deep trouble, have turned to Lahiri Mahasaya for help, feeling a close kinship with this man who successfully fitted two entirely different worlds together into a unified whole.

The fifth in the chain of gurus was Swami Sri Yukteswar (1855-1936). He was a disciple of Mahasaya and was trained by him for his own guruhood. By definition he was a *Jnanatavar*, or "incarnation of wisdom." He received his Kriya initiation from his master; later he was personally visited by Babaji. He was a stern taskmaster and a strict disciplinarian, yet one possessed of a sense of humor. It was in his ashram that for nearly a decade he trained the gifted and inspired youth who was eventually to become his successor. He initiated Yogananda into the swami order and motivated him to take up his mission in the western world. An extended account of the life of Swami Yukteswar appears in *Autobiography of a Yogi*. An indication of his spiritual status is found in the fact that he was able to appear to his disciple after his own death to give him further instruction.

Paramhansa Yogananda (1893-1952), disciple of Sri Yukteswar, was the sixth of the gurus. He stated that he was the last of his line and to date no one has presumed to question that statement. His greatest disciple is Sri Daya Mata, the president of the Self Realization Fellowship. Others who knew him well, and who were his direct devotees, include Brother Anandamoy of the SRF and Swami Kriyananda, the man who was to realize his guru's dream of a successful spiritual community inspired and guided by the teachings of the great yoga masters.

Chapter Three

The Evolution of Donald Walters

It was hot in Lost Angeles on the afternoon of 12 September, 1948. In the Hollywood church of the Self Realization Fellowship, which he had founded twenty eight years before, Paramhansa Yogananda sat in his study, doing his best to keep up with a crowded and unrelenting schedule. His mission to the West had reached such a level of success it had almost engulfed him in the process. He literally did not have a minute to spare when he was informed that there was a young man in the church who wanted to see him.

There was nothing very unusual in that request. People came to see him all the time; some to question, some to interview, some to pledge fervent support to the point of embarrassment. His book, *Autobiography of a Yogi*, had become an international classic in its field, a position it still occupies. Two weeks previously a lady had arrived unannounced from Sweden; after having read the book she had flown at once to California to prostrate herself before its author. Yogananda had regretfully declined to see her; his time had simply been booked solidly for the following two and a half months. Besides, God had not indicated to him that this excellent lady had any special role to play in the work he had been given to do.

There were several others also waiting to see him, some of whom had been doing so literally for weeks. It was a major concession to the newcomer that he had been announced at all.

Certainly he was not an imposing figure. He was dressed in a Palm Beach suit under the mistaken belief that such was the preferred garb in Los Angeles. He had just spent four full days and four nights riding in a transcontinental bus. He had discovered and read *Autobiography of a Yogi* in New York and despite the fact that much of what the book contained he found hard to believe, he had been sufficiently moved by the rest to leave almost at once for California.

From his reading he had concluded that the great Indian master would be found at the hermitage in Encinitas, a small city well down the coastline toward San Diego. He had gone there immediately, arriving in the late afternoon almost totally exhausted. After being fortified by a night's sleep in a hotel room, he had walked to the hermitage and a hoped-for appointment with destiny. Then he had learned that Yogananda was not there.

Instead of the interview for which he had been so desperately hoping, he had been given advice: it would be to his benefit to study the lessons. That was the first he had heard of them; quite reasonably he asked how long they would take to complete.

He was told that four years would suffice. There were almost two hundred of them and they were doled out to subscribers at a rate of one a week.

Four years!

He was offered one more piece of information: Yogananda was at the Hollywood church where it might be possible to hear him conduct a service. That definitely was news: up until that moment the young man had not been at all sure that Hollywood had any churches. He spoke his thanks and left at once for the church at 4860 Sunset Boulevard.

It took him most of the day to get there. When he finally did arrive and present himself, he was told that the Master, as Yogananda was commonly called by then, was totally engaged for an indefinite period. At first disappointed, the young man prayerfully asked for the help of God. A moment later a secretary approached him and said that she would at least pass in the word that he was there.

To Paramhansa Yogananda the God that he served so devoutly had more than one aspect: He was at once both the Heavenly Father and the Divine Mother—a typical essence of eastern thought. As he applied himself to his work, he received an unexpected enlightenment. By his own statement, Divine Mother made clear Her wish that he receive this newcomer. Despite the many other things he had to do, he obediently sent out word that the young man was to be shown in.

A few moments later the slender twenty-two year old stood before the fifty-five year old *Premavatar* or Incarnation of Love and declared himself. "I want to be your disciple," he said.

"What is your name?"

"Donald Walters."

Gently the Indian sage led the conversation. By that time his command of English was fluent, if accented. In addition to that, he had an insight into character and motivations that was at times disconcerting to those who were closest to him. He could not be fooled by anyone about anything. He always knew. And he knew that this latest arrival who stood before him was destined to go far.

As the conversation progressed he learned that the youthful candidate had been born in Rumania where his father had been an oil geologist. Later the Walters family had traveled to many different European countries. While growing up, young Donald had displayed a gift for languages and had acquired several with no apparent difficulty. He had gone through the usual process of education in his own country, but early in his still very young life had discovered that the conventional pyramid climbing in business and society was not for him. Since Yogananda as a young boy had practiced meditation himself up to seven hours each day, he understood perfectly.

He also understood when young Walters told him that upon reading the *Autobiography* he had at once sworn off meat, fish and fowl for life. Twenty two is a very young age to decide to become a monk, particularly a yogic one, but Donald Walters was ready. Yogananda knew that too. He made the decision to which Divine Mother had guided him.Taking his young visitor outside he announced, "We have a new brother."

As of that moment things had been happening in the life of young Mr. Walters with astonishing speed. He had sought a berth as a common seaman, messman, and wiper, but before he

was called to assume any of those duties he read the
Autobiography and the vibrations that arose from its pages
were enough to fix his mind with almost massive
determination in a totally new direction. As he read the text he
became aware of several split infinitives, but he was not in a
mood to be critical. There was something there that seemed to
fill his whole being and he knew he would have to leave for
California almost at once. In view of subsequent events, it is
quite possible, perhaps even likely, that Divine Mother had
a hand in that too.

His conversion was immediate and complete. Yoga does
not require its devotees to become vegetarians, but since it was
suggested, he accepted the practice promptly and without
reservation. On the long bus trip to the Coast, as the weary
days and nights took their toll of him, his spirit never faltered.
For at the other end would be, he most fervently hoped,
Yogananda himself and a totally new life as his dedicated
disciple. It never occurred to him for a moment to look back.

He knew almost nothing about the spiritual path he was
about to adopt or many of its tenets. In his own words, "My
heart and soul were converted indeed, but my intellect lagged
far behind. Reincarnation, karma, superconsciousness, divine
ecstasy, the astral world, masters, gurus, breathing exercises,
vegetarianism, health foods, *sabikalpa* and *nirbikalpa
samadhi*, Christ Consciousness... for me these were all new and
staggering concepts; a week or two before I hadn't even known
they existed."

Reverend Bernard, the alternate minister at the
Hollywood SRF church, took Donald and another disciple in
his car to the bus station where Master's newest follower had
left his modest luggage. Then the small party proceeded
toward Pasadena and Mount Washington, atop which the Self
Realization Fellowship had its headquarters in what had once
been a fashionable summit hotel. As the car ended its
laborious, twisting climb up the narrow road and finally drove
into the grounds, Donald Walters looked about him and felt
that he was home. Even more important to him, he had found
his guru.

In common with some other terms of very specific meaning, the word *guru* has been liberally used in a much broader and more common context. Almost any sort of a teacher has become known as a guru and if perhaps the instruction he gives tends to be exotic, the term has struck even closer until a faint aura of eccentricity has become associated both with the word itself and with those to whom it is applied.

Any given person can have many teachers and in the normal course events will—from high school instructors, to college professors, and then on to specialists in scuba diving, tennis, languages, home economics, music or sky diving, as tastes may dictate. But a person can have only one guru. And, according to long-established tradition, he does not need to seek him out; when the time comes that anyone needs and is ready for his guru, God will send His chosen representative to him.

Strictly speaking a guru is a spiritual guide, but the term goes farther than that. The relationship is a permanent one. Once the bond of guru and disciple has been formed, it is never to be broken: in this life or in any that may follow. Even after a guru has left this earth, he continues to guide and care for his disciples from another plane. And just as Christ appeared to His disciples after His resurrection, there are many accounts of great gurus who have manifested themselves after their own deaths to continue their roles as guides and mentors.

It is therefore of the utmost importance to any spiritually-minded individual that he or she find his true and right guru, the one divinely appointed to undertake the task. Paramhansa Yogananda has been accepted by tens of thousands as their guru. No reasonable person familiar with him and his life's work would deny him the right to that status.

For the next four years Donald Walters continued to live at Mount Washington or wherever else his guru chose to take him. Perhaps because of his very youthful appearance Yogananda instructed him to grow a beard, and he did. He applied himself to his studies with the dedication of a true devotee; the life of a monk following in the footsteps of the great Indian masters suited him to perfection. His parents, who were perhaps passively waiting for him to come home, were somewhat less enthusiastic.

In due course he was ordained and began to give services in the same church where he had first been accepted into the Fellowship. He still stuck to a vegetarian diet, mastered the sometimes fiendishly difficult yoga postures, became an adept at meditation and schooled himself in some of the Indian languages, including Sanskrit. He was present at the gala dinner given at the Los Angeles Biltmore Hotel in honor of Indian ambassador Biney R. Sen on 7 March, 1952. On that occasion Paramhansa Yogananda delivered a very well received address; at the end of which he slipped to the floor and entered *mahasamadhi*, a yogi's final conscious exit from his body. His remains were quietly removed to Forest Lawn Memorial Park where after the passage of some time, they showed not the slightest signs of change.

To the members of the Self Realization Fellowship the death of Yogananda took from them the physical presence of their guru, but not his spirit or his continuing guidance. He had himself stated that he was the last of his line of gurus, and that he would have no direct successor. After three decades the Fellowship's devotion to him has been unfaltering and they publish his photograph every Saturday with the religious announcements in the *Los Angeles Times*.

Mr. James Lynn, a sincere and very advanced disciple of Yogananda, succeeded him as president of the Fellowship. One of his key aides was the dedicated Sri Daya Mata. As Faye Wright she had come to Yogananda a girl of seventeen. A very gifted and deeply spiritual person, she had chosen to sit all night with the body of her guru after his passing, keeping a vigil. During the still, small hours a visible tear appeared on his cheek; with her handkerchief she lifted it away.

Years later, after she had become the Reverend Mother of the Self Realization Fellowship, Daya Mata faced a critical decision in her work. By her own account at her time of greatest stress Yogananda appeared to her in his physical form. She touched his feet (a traditional mark of respect in India) and found them as solid as her own. Although he did not speak, she understood his meaning and found the solution to her dilemma. James Lynn also received a visit and on that occasion Yogananda spoke in his natural voice. There had never been any doubt whatever in the minds of his followers, but these miraculous reappearances of the dead Master, and some others known to have occurred, confirimed to them for all time that he had been a true messenger of God.

With singleness of purpose the Fellowship was determined to carry on. One substantial job that needed doing was a reorganization of the offices; with another disciple Donald Walters undertook the work anticipating that it would require two weeks. A year and a half later they were still at it. What emerged was a much better operating system that would be able to handle the anticipated continuing growth of the Fellowship.

In 1955 James Lynn, the president, died and after an appropriate interval Daya Mata was elected to succeed him. Her selection was a popular one, many feeling that she was the best possible choice. On 20 August of the same year Donald Walters and three others took their final vows of renunciation and became full monks. At that time spiritual names were bestowed upon them. To Walters, who had been appointed chief minister of the Hollywood church, Daya Mata gave the significant name Kriyananda, which, loosely translated, means heavenly joy through Kriya Yoga (about which more later). Through the Fellowship's connections with the ancient swami order of India this entrance into *sannya*, final renunciation and a total dedication to the service of God, carried with it admission to the *giri*, or mountain branch. At age twenty-nine the one-time enrolled seaman was supplanted by the bearded young ordained monk; Donald Walters had become Swami Kriyananda.

Three years later Kriyananda left for his first visit to India where he was to remain for nearly four years. He swiftly acquired a fluent command of Bengali. He delivered many lectures and within a short time acquired a growing reputation as the American yogi. Although he was still a very young man, under the inspiration of absolute dedication he had matured rapidly. He had exceptional gifts as a speaker despite his still persistent natural inclination for privacy and seclusion. He gratified this in part by spending a month in a tiny cave in the Himalaya where he devoted himself very largely to meditation.

In 1960 he was called back to Mount Washington. There he received a substantial reward for his labors: he was elected to the Board of Directors of the Self Realization Fellowship and to the office of First Vice President. By this time almost all of the principals within the Fellowship knew that in Kriyananda they had an original. He did not conform to any of the well-established patterns and, like so many others of whom that may be said, there were a few who wished that it were otherwise. Certainly he was remarkably versatile. He could speak publicly in any of several languages. He sang well, played a variety of instruments, and composed music of engaging quality. He could write with clarity on a wide variety of topics. And he was a more than competent organizer.

The Fellowship sent him back to India for another two years where he continued his work of lecturing and developing the Indian affiliant of the Fellowship, the Yogoda Satsanga Society of India. Among his other duties he was directed to locate a site for a spiritual center and shrine in the vicinity of New Delhi. This task proved extraordinarily difficult; when he did at last locate a very desirable parcel, and discovered that it could be obtained at a surprisingly favorable price, he went into action. When obstacles appeared in the form of technicalities, he managed to secure an audience with Nehru and enlisted his help. The difficulties promptly began to disappear.

Then, quite unexpectedly, Kriyananda's efforts were denounced by his fellow directors in California as separatism and he was summoned back to the United States. He was asked to come to New York, rather than to California where almost all of the church's activities were centered. Here, with a note that the lady called Tara was one of the top ranking members of the Self Realization Fellowship at the time, it seems best to let Kriyananda tell the story in his own words:

A telegram in July, 1962, summoned me to New York City. There, at Idylwild, Tara and Daya Mata met me. We took a taxi to the Hilton Hotel, opposite the Penn Station. The next morning I found shoved under my door a thick envelope containing a letter some thirty pages long, denouncing me and telling me I was through in SRF.

Later that morning I got to speak at length to the two of them. I pleaded to be allowed even to wash dishes for the rest of my life, just for the chance of being able to continue serving my Guru.

'Never!' Tara replied; it was she who led the meeting. 'The least chance you get, you'll worm your way to the top again.

'From now on,' she continued, 'you must never tell anyone that you are Master's disciple. You must never again set foot on any SRF property. If you contact any SRF member, we'll publically expose your countless acts of treachery.' In conclusion, she informed me, 'We're tired of playing nursemaid to Kriyananda!'

'But it's just not TRUE, what you've been saying about me!' I'd been given no chance to plead my own case.

'I don't want your opinions! I have the power to know people's true natures. I know you better than you know yourself.'

They gave me a letter to sign stating that I resigned from the vice-presidency of SRF, and from the SRF Board of Directors. I signed it.*

Before the meeting concluded, Tara heaped enough vitriolic criticism on the earnest young monk to drive any average person out of his mind. When it was at last over he was left, at thirty six, with nowhere to go, no marketable skills, no job, no friends, and no home.

Under severe emotional pain Kriyananda's first thought was to return to India where he could find Himalayan solitude and, possibly, peace. He was denied a visa on the grounds that he was a suspected C.I.A. agent and, for good measure, a Christian missionary in disguise.

He had one thing left—his guru. During the following two weeks, in intense shock, he remained in seclusion asking in prayer for his Master's help and guidance. Then he left for the West Coast and sanctuary in the home of his parents. Like many others who have suffered severe traumas in their lives, he thought it might be best if he were to die. But when he prayed

*From a letter to the author, 29 December, 1980. Kriyananda later stated verbally that Daya Mata had only consented to this after incessant pounding by Tara at last overcame her own vigorous objections.

to his guru, he received back a resounding *no!*.

The agonies he endured the following months and years need not be detailed here. He has told the story himself in *The Path: Autobiography of a Western Yogi.* (Available in both hard cover and paperback from Ananda Publications, Nevada City, California 95959.) It may be noted that he took refuge for six months in a Catholic monastery, but at the end of that time it was thought best all around that he should leave. After doing so officially he remained long enough to give the Retreat Master Kriya initiation.

One evening in September 1962, while living with his parents, he reluctantly accepted a dinner invitation at a neighbor's residence. There he met Dr. and Mrs. Haridas Chaudhuri who had come originally from Calcutta. When he conversed with them in fluent Bengali, they were suitably amazed. He had been introduced to them by his parents as "our son, Donald"; nothing had been said beyond that. When the Chaudhuris asked for an explanation of his unexpected language ability, he mentioned his monastic name.

"Kriyananda!" they cried in unexpected delight, for they owned his recording of Yogananda's chants. As instant rapport was established. Dr. Chaudhuri, it turned out, was the founder and spiritual director of the respected Cultural Integration Fellowship of San Francisco. From that evening forward the Chaudhuris befriended Kriyananda and offered him a home in their ashram.

Kriyananda lived with them for more than a year. When Dr. Chaudhuri was suddenly stricken with a heart attack, Kriyananda replaced him in his pulpit during his recuperation. Gradually he began to give classes in yoga and meditation, earning some sorely needed income. Meanwhile he searched the country and Mexico for any sort of a religious retreat where he could hide himself from the world, but on every occasion he was sooner or later frustrated. Then, at long last, it came to him that his guru, to whom he had been praying so faithfully, was trying to tell him something. His problem was that he didn't yet know what it was.

Five years after he received the incredible letter in New

York he was still seeking a place of permanent seclusion. But he had begun to publish and his writings were attracting attention. Not once, either verbally or in print, did he speak against the organization that had, he thought, taken from him his life's career.

He continued to lecture on Indian philosophy and yoga to ever increasing audiences. Because he had been welcomed so warmly into the swami order in India, he made proper use of that title. (Had he remained within the SRF he would have been Brother Kriyananda, but he had been expressly forbidden to call himself that.)

In January 1967 he quite unexpectedly learned of a piece of property in north central California, near Nevada City, that might exactly suit his purposes. Furthermore, his lectures were bringing in enough income to make its purchase a possibility. The price was only $250 an acre which, for California land even in a remote region, was remarkably cheap. A total of 172 acres was available to be divided up, if all went well, among four buyers. The little group included two well-known poets, Allen Ginsberg and Gary Snyder, and Richard Baker, the president of the Zen Center in San Francisco.

Shortly thereafter the four men drove to see the property. In Kriyananda's words, "Our trip took us far out into the countryside. The last three miles were dirt road, deeply rutted, and barely passable after the winter rains. The altitude was 3,000 feet. The air was fresh. The property was rolling, wooded, serene, and gave onto several beautiful views of distant snow-capped mountains."

As he wandered about, "feeling out" the land, one particular section attracted him very strongly. It had an eastern exposure which, in yoga, is significant. It seemed to Kriyananda that his guru had already blessed this particular parcel, but there were three others to be considered and a conflict of choice was quite possible. If that were to occur, then as the newest member of the group, it would be up to him to give way.

Quite remarkably, each of the potential landowners felt attracted to a different section of the property. Kriyananda's choice was not contested. In his words, "I could not help feeling that it was for this place that God had made me wait all those years. At last my search was ended."

In that he was fully correct. He had indeed found a place where he could build something modest to live in and then spend the rest of his days in quiet contemplation and prayer, passively serving his God and his guru. The site was indeed close to ideal, but Kriyananda still did not know what it was that his guru was to require of him.

Chapter Four

The Stalwarts—John Novak

When Kriyananda first stood on the piece of land he had discovered in northern California, five years had passed since he had departed so abruptly from the Self Realization Fellowship. During that long and painful interval two ideas had been stored away in his mind. He greatly wanted a place of retreat where he could be by himself and live the life of a monk according to the vows he had taken and which, to him, were still in force. And, if possible, he wanted to live in a dome.

In a certain sense his separation from the SRF had been one-sided: he had been ejected from the Fellowship without ceremony, but despite his great hurt, he had not allowed himself to become embittered. It was his guru's organization and therefore he still gave it his loyalty. That was the kind of forgiveness Yogananda had taught and he intended to follow his master's path to the end.

The dome idea had come to him in India in 1962. It had seemed to him that a half sphere arcing overhead would provide a close to ideal spiritual environment. A lofty ceiling, he reasoned, would encourage and stimulate lofty thoughts. There were, however, some practical problems. Domes are intricate things to construct and very expensive in comparison to ordinary structures. They are necessarily round while almost all standard furniture is basically rectangular. Also, if a second floor is desired, the inward slope of a dome will constrict it with ever-increasing severity.

Practical or not, Kriyananda wanted a dome. Under it he would be able to sit calmly in expansive meditation. He also wanted in time to build a temple as well, and that would be a dome too.

Since he had been carefully saving the funds earned by his teaching, he began to think in terms of construction. But there was no local builder ready and qualified to put up a large-sized dome. Kriyananda therefore decided that the only thing would be to build it himself. When he mentioned this project to one of his students, she asked if he was familiar with the geodesic dome, the remarkable invention of Buckminster Fuller.

He was not and therefore went to see some. He found one squat shape that looked like a toadstool and was discouraged; then a professor friend showed him a geodesic "sun dome" that he was erecting in his back yard. It was inexpensive, beautiful in its apparent simplicity, and seemed to be easy to construct.

It was the answer! With enthusiasm Kriyananda went to work at his building site. He laid out and constructed a sturdy platform of the right shape despite the fact that, by his own admission, he was not a carpenter. By the time he had cut the struts exactly to the correct angles, assembled them into triangles, and then covered each such component with heavy plastic, he had put in months of heavy, but inspired labor. He was determined to finish his retreat before the end of the year. A few of his students gave him some help.

He fitted his triangles together in Mr. Fuller's intricate geometry and saw his dome begin to take shape. It rose high and curved inward, just as it should. Like an arch under construction, it needed only a few cap pieces to make it all lock together into a firm structure. Before they could be fitted, a great gust of wind blew up from the valley below and attacked the nearly complete dome with one powerful swoop. Down it came in toto, a jumbled confusion of splintered triangles and torn plastic.

The wind had been tough, but Kriyananda was determined to be tougher. He began his reconstruction at once and when he had at last finished, his dome stood complete: exquisite and beautiful in its airy grace. And so it remained until the first strong storm came through; as it fell once again into shattered fragments, Kriyananda walked away without even looking back.

A few weeks later, still undaunted, he tried again. This

time he screwed his triangles together with strong metal plates so that no likely wind could possible tear them apart. When he had at last completed the hard and laborous job, he left for San Francisco with a firm sense of accomplishment; his long awaited place of retreat for solitary meditation was at last his. As soon as he had completed his teaching obligations, he returned to the mountains to begin his seclusion. This time the heavy winds had picked up his dome whole, whirled it about, and deposited its fragments across the surrounding flora.

Kiryananda stood there, looked about him, and accepted the will of God. Somewhat gingerly he climbed up onto what was once again an open platform, seated himself facing the east, and closed his eyes. He had built three domes and all of them had been mercilessly destroyed. Many long months of hard physical labor had been wiped out and almost all of his money was gone. He sat very still, turned his mind inward, and surrounded by the wreckage of his hopes and aspirations, he had a joyous meditation. During it he received a message: his first task was not to build himself a home, but a temple. And to make use of it, there would have to be a community—one dedicated to yoga and to the noble goal of world brotherhood.

To attempt any such project, he knew, might well cost him twenty five years of his life and he looked for a way out of such a commitment of his resources. Possibly he would be able to help others to found such a community; he might even serve as its spiritual director. He was still looking forward to seclusion and a withdrawn life.

Because he had no other choice, he went back to full time teaching. He had lost his home and had nothing left with which to build another. But as the old year gave way to the new, silently and invisibly his guru seemed to return to him and to give him guidance, as he had so often done when they had been together in life. Kriyananda knew then that he was going to found a community, and lead it, and that it would be called Ananda.

To young John Novak his native state of Minnesota was

primarily a place from which to escape. Despite its beauty and 10,000 lakes, he did not cotton to its very cold winters or to its state bird, the mosquito. As soon as he had completed high school, he set off with a friend to see something of the fabled land of California. When he had his first encounter with San Francisco, he literally fell in love with the city. When he returned to Minnesota, he took with him the conviction that the magical metropolis with the great bridges would some day be his home.

The idea remained firmly fixed in his mind during the four years of his college education while he studied psychology and took his B.A. degree. The day after his graduation he set out to return to the city that had captured his heart. He very much wanted a new life and, to a considerable degree, a new direction. He had been an Episcopalian more or less by birth, but from the time he had been sixteen, he had turned agnostic, Episcopalianism being too enclosing for him. In his own words, what he was seeking was "a deeper direction in life."

With that objective in mind, he did a great deal of reading. One of the works he found interesting was Yogananda's *Autobiography of a Yogi*. While in a bookstore, he encountered a man who told him that although Yogananda was dead, a direct disciple of his was living and teaching in the city. That, Novak found, was of real interest; he made a decision to look the man up. On a Sunday morning in January 1967, accompanied by his brother in law, but without the benefit of an appointment, he knocked on the door of the man's apartment.

Kriyananda opened it, welcomed his two unexpected visitors, and promptly put them to work. He was getting out a mailing and he could use some help. When that task was completed, the three of them went on a picnic in the park. Kriyananda took his guitar and sang some of his spiritual songs. (He has a very agreeable and well-trained voice.) John Novak was attracted to him at once; on the spot he enrolled himself in the classes Kriyananda was giving on the yoga postures and how to meditate.

After locating a job as a social worker in order to support

himself, Novak continued to take all of the classes that Kriyananda was offering. He also began to attend the Thursday evening satsangs. These were spiritually oriented social gatherings at which ideas and aspirations could be discussed among people of similar interests. The classes were doing well with enrollments of from 25 to 40 students each. Soon John was assisting, serving as cashier, selling books, and helping beginning students with the yoga postures. He had not made a firm commitment, but his sincere interest had very definitely been awakened.

He had learned enough of the yogic way so that he was meditating each morning and evening as well as attending most of the services that Kriyananda was giving. As Christmas 1967 approached, he was given Kriya initiation. He took the vows that are part of that ceremony and advanced much closer to total commitment. He was thoroughly involved, but not yet ready to dedicate his life to the Path.

Meanwhile he had accompanied Kriyananda on a number of visits to his retreat under construction in Nevada County. A well and a water tower were the first improvements put in with the help of a few others of the swami's students. Most of them found that they had no real taste for physical labor and ceased coming. Some questions arose between the other three members of the Bald Mountain Association concerning the ultimate use Kriyananda was planning to make of his share of the property. In particular, Richard Baker, who was erecting a zen temple imported from Japan on his own sector, wanted the whole area to remain as secluded and quiet as possible. Even the limited development envisioned by the swami did not meet with his unqualified approval.

In the city the enrollment in Kriyananda's classes continued to grow, but many of his students turned away from the patient path of meditation to seek mind expansion through drugs instead. John Novak was sensitive to all this as he continued to offer his help. He assisted in the construction of the first dome and after it was destroyed, he went to work with Kriyananda on the second. He shared the crushing disappointment when that too was torn apart by unanticipated high winds. When the swami found the strength to begin again for the third time, John was there to give his physical and moral support.

One noon, when work had ceased long enough to eat some of the food that had been brought, Kriyananda went off and sat by himself, his back turned toward the others. As John ate, concern mounted within him that the determined spirit of his mentor had broken at last. So much hard work had been done, and there was so little to show for it except acute disaster.

He could have sat there, but that was not his way. Instead he got to his feet and quietly approached the man whose optimistic hopes had been so effectively stiffled, if not extinguished altogether. Perhaps a few words of encouragement, and of understanding, would help. Or just the offer of continuing friendship; he was prepared to give of his best.

Then, as he drew close enough, he heard Kriyananda speaking very quietly to himself. "Oh, joy. Oh, joy!"

No one was intended to hear. But John Novak did hear. And wonder welled up within him that any man faced with such adversity could still find joy in what he was doing.

That settled it: in those moments his commitment was made and he knew that Ananda, whatever it was to become, would be the focal point of the rest of his life.

Chapter Five

The Farm—Seva

By the early summer of 1968 Kriyananda had developed plans for a Meditation Retreat on his property, one that would be available to a limited number of people and would, hopefully, produce some revenue toward the eventual development of a full community. He had also reached the sound conclusion that if he still wanted domes for the use of the future retreatants, he would need some professional help in their construction.

By combining his earning from teaching yoga, some gifts from friends, and some stock holdings his father had given him over the years, he had been able to assemble $16,000, a sum he felt would be enough to do the job. He found a carpenter who assured him that with a little help he would be able to put up two solid domes, one for the temple and the other to be a common dome for general use, in a matter of two weeks. Kriyananda engaged him to do the job.

The contractor hired two men to help him. In addition, a number of the swami's students were willing to work for minimum wages in order to enjoy a summer living in the woods. Everyone went to work on schedule, but at the end of the stated two weeks, not even the foundations had been completed. This is perhaps understandable since, in addition to the two main domes, a small bathhouse, office, and another attempt at a home for Kriyananda were all under construction. It was then evident that at least another two months would be required to finish everything. Long before that time, the swami once more ran out of money.

Hopefully he went to the bank; dejectedly he left. To the bank officials a yoga teacher had not seemed to be a good risk.

When it became clear that another $12,000 would be required, and no further funds were in sight, the chief carpenter and his leading assistant quit. At that point the local lumber company put a lien on the land. Several thousand dollars were due and the supplier was taking no chances.

Kriyananda called on his creditors and obtained an agreement from them to accept partial payments on a monthly basis. He committed himself for $2500 a month, certain that in one way or another, God would help. God did; more students than ever enrolled in the swami's classes. Friends came through nobly to help out. Every month, often with pennies to spare, he made his agreed upon payments.

The lumber company, however, was still not satisfied. Despite the fact that he was receiving the partial payments promptly, the owner tried to force a foreclosure.

Two days later Kriyananda presented a slide show as part of his fund-raising effort. When he had finished a stranger approached him and offered to make a small donation. Grateful for even five or ten dollars, the swami accepted. The man then handed over a check for $3,000.00, strong evidence to Kriyananda that his guru had not deserted him.

In the morning he called the lumber company and informed the owner that he had the funds to meet his bill in full. However, he added, since the owner had broken the agreement, the swami proposed letting him incur the maximum legal costs and then paying him at the very last moment.

Aware that he had been outmaneuvered, the lumber yard owner offered a substantial discount in exchange for prompt payment. Kriyananda settled the reduced bill in full, met some other obligations, and then counted what was left. He had one dollar and thirty seven cents.

That marked the turning point. Before the end of the year the Meditation Retreat had been completed and this time the domes stayed securely in place. Through the generosity of many people who made contributions, it was very nearly paid off. By that time five men and two women were living permanently on the grounds. They were camped out and winter was coming, but no one seemed to mind. High hopes for the future Ananda community were strong in their minds.

In November Kriyananda asked John Novak if he would care to resign his job as a social worker in order to join him as a full-time assistant. There was one major drawback; he could only propose a very small salary.

The offer crystalized Novak's commitment to the yogic path and sealed his future. "I was always a pretty frugal fellow," he said in discussing the incident, "so I accepted."

The swami was not quite through. "How do you like the name Jyotish?" he asked, "In Sanskrit it means 'inner light'."

The bestowing of spiritual names was a well established tradition long followed in India and in many other places, including the Self Realization Fellowship. John Novak realized that he was being offered initiation into a new elite, of which he would become the first member.

"That's fine with me," he answered, and Jyotish he became.

For a single girl Sonia Wiberg was doing exceptionally well. She had a very good job as accountant to a firm of architects. She had an attention-getting sports car which she drove happily about San Francisco and its environs. Also she was very attractive. Men liked her and she, in turn, liked them. Few of her contemporaries would deny that she had it made.

But despite all of the external signs of a highly gratifying life style, she could not rid herself of the inner feeling that something was missing. She was one of those relatively rare people who have both a spiritual need and a definite urge to satisfy it. Therefore, when she heard about Kriyananda, she decided to invest an evening to hear what he had to say.

Eastern philosophy and religion was something very new to her, but as she listened to the bearded American swami talk, something very strong stirred within her. It was early in 1968; the place was the North Point Apartments in San Francisco. By the time the lecture was over, Sonia knew that she had found something. She talked with the swami and signed up to take some of his classes.

Her conversion to the yogic path was swift and secure.

Within a very short time she knew she had found what she had been seeking. She offered her services to keep the financial accounts for the proposed Ananda project; her suggestion was accepted at once. She went to work with a will and within a short time, when real activity began at the property in Nevada County, she became the swami's principal aide in San Francisco.

Meanwhile she advanced very rapidly in the study of yoga. She practiced the postures which, to so many people *are* yoga, and carefully studied the philosophies and techniques of the ancient science. She became skilled in meditation, as her dedication deepened even further. Before too many months had passed Kriyananda gave her Kriya initiation; she took the vows willingly and eagerly. When the construction project at the Meditation Retreat began to run out of money, she donated $2000 of her savings to help meet the outstanding bills.

Almost from the first it was understood that as soon as Ananda became a reality, she would move there, continuing her role as accountant and, in many respects, financial manager. The swami bestowed on her the spiritual name of Seva, which in Sanskrit means 'service.' Not for a moment did she look behind her; she only looked forward to the community that was to be, where others of equal spiritual conviction could live together in the mutual sharing that the Indians called *satsang*. She had many friends, but proposals of marriage did not interest her at all. Kriyananda knew that he had found a pillar, one who would be as valuable in her way as Jyotish was in his, and it gave him a great sense of comfort and joy.

When the winter broke and spring came, the Meditation Retreat was the scene of considerable activity. The first classes on the property were begun and some simple cabins were erected for the use of visiting retreatants. A dormitory was begun to house additional students. Obviously the Retreat could not attract many students without providing some form of accommodations in lieu of camping out. Meanwhile a few feelers were put out to find suitable property for the community to be, but nothing of a promising nature appeared.

Kriyananda was in San Francisco when he received an urgent letter from Richard Baker of the Bald Mountain Association. In unequivocal terms Baker wrote from Japan, "Don't do any more building until I get back." It was then June and Baker was not due back until September, at which time the better part of the summer would be gone.

The swami was desperate to know what to do. All of the momentum he had generated could not be stopped dead without doing the whole Ananda dream irreparable harm. But to ignore Baker's letter was impossible, according to their agreement. It is not recorded whether or not he employed the yogi's standard method of imploring help by chanting "Aum, Guru; Aum, Guru," but a series of events began almost at once which, when viewed in retrospect, seem to have fallen far outside the normal boundaries of probability.

On the day before he received Baker's letter, Kriyananda had encountered a doctor friend who had told him of a real estate man who was offering some property, "in the same general area as the Retreat."

The next day, on his way to the Retreat after receiving Baker's discouraging letter, Kriyananda stopped at the doctor friend's office in Sacramento. While he was waiting, a real estate salesman came in full of enthusiasm for a fine piece of property he had listed in Nevada County. To be polite, the swami asked where it was. The salesman produced a map; the location was just six miles down the road from the Retreat.

He was, of course, the same real estate man who had been mentioned to Kriyananda the previous day. The swami asked when he could see this piece of land. He was told that the very desirable property had been subdivided into forty acre parcels, but if he wanted to see them, he could that same afternoon.

With high hopes Kriyananda left with the salesman, blocking out of his mind the unhappy fact that he had no funds at all with which to purchase anything.

The property in question was called the Sylvester farm; the owner was selling because he was a victim of terminal cancer. It was not a very prepossessing holding as it stood, since it had been used principally to raise pigs. However, as a site for a cooperative community it did seem to hold some promise.

With complete optimism Kriyananda began to select parcels to buy. He chose one reputed to have the best spring and a spectacular view of the Yuba River a thousand feet below (*Ayodhya* at the present time) and some six other 40 acre pieces of the property, a total of 285 acres.

The salesman computed the total price to be $206,000 not including the interest charges which would run the total cost up well over a quarter million. The good news was the down payment: only $13,500 would be required, but that sum would have to be produced almost immediately.

With every show of confidence Kriyananda agreed, certain that his guru would not have revealed the property to him without at the same time providing some means for its purchase. At two in the morning the salesman went to the real estate office and took the selected parcels off the board.

In the morning, when the other salesman came in, there was a grand scramble for the Sylvester property, but Kriyananda had his 72 hour option. He was not there; he was fervently on the telephone, calling everyone he knew who might be able to help with the essential down payment.

By Monday morning he had received enough pledges to call the broker and inform him that the deal was on. In so doing he automatically obligated himself to come up with a monthly payment of approximately $2000 for the next ten years, in addition to other costs. It was probably a good buy at the time, despite the fact that the owner had been trying to sell the same property for $90,000.00 the year before without success.

Of those who pledged their help, almost none came through with checks, but somehow Kriyananda did manage to put together the down payment and delivered the funds to the broker on time.

Once the deal was concluded and the farm definitely sold, Mr. Sylvester began to experience a miraculous recovery. To the complete amazement of the medical people in charge, from a supposedly terminal cancer condition he went on the mend until he fully recovered his health. At that point he tried to regain ownership of the farm, but the escrow had long since been closed.

As soon as possession was granted, there was a general exodus from the Meditation Retreat to the farm. The first of the new tenants arrived to take up residence on the property on the Fourth of July, 1969. They found very little of material value or usefulness awaiting them in the form of improvements, but the spirit of the first inhabitants was, by their own account, "wonderful."

For the time being Ananda had all the land it needed. The promise of great things to come radiated everywhere. There were not too many people, but that too would change. Legally the new community had been classified as a church camp, which put it under the sole auspices of the County Health Department. This arrangement gave it a great deal of freedom.

It appeared to everyone that Ananda's Prosperity Prayer had indeed come true:

> "The sunshine of Divine prosperity has just burst through my dark skies of limitations. I am God's child. What He has, I have."

It is just as well that those who had moved onto the property with such enthusiasm did not know what lay ahead of them.

Chapter Six

The Hard Winter—Jaya, Devi, and Binay

By the year 1969 a substantial "back to the land" movement had developed within the United States. It was spawned by many things: the general discontent with the direction of the economy, student protests against various established institutions, the Vietnam war, and a growing alienation with the existing urban living conditions. For people in many different age and economic brackets the idea of turning to the countryside where they could live more freely and perhaps grow some of their own food held a considerable attraction.

At the same time in San Francisco, and elsewhere, the drug culture was strongly entrenched. Those who were addicted to it were also anxious for a change of scene. To them a rural environment seemed to promise less interference with their way of life and a greater freedom of choice than the cities were willing to offer.

The desire on the part of so many to escape from urban living stresses, air pollution and constantly growing crime accounted in large part for the founding of hundreds of new communities and communes throughout the country. Most of these were short lived and for a variety of reasons disappeared within a few weeks. When word of the new place called Ananda reached the grapevine, prospective recruits and members began to appear in almost alarming numbers.

The atmosphere at the Meditation Retreat was already well defined: it was a strictly spiritual environment intended for those who sought a closer communion with God through the teachings of Paramhansa Yogananda. It was off to a very good start: even during its first season the classes offered there in

51

yoga postures, meditation, philosophy and practical spiritual living were well filled, largely by students from Kriyananda's classes in the San Francisco Bay area.

Because of the urgent need to raise funds, he remained in the city where he continued to teach during the week. Once his obligations were met he would hurry back to the Retreat for the weekend. He began to conduct Sunday services in the temple and, in the words of a resident of the time, "They were wonderful."

Insofar as he was concerned, nothing was going to stop the flow of energy that was going into Ananda, particularly since the acquisition of the Farm had provided much needed *Lebensraum* for the community. To take charge of the new property he commissioned a trio of trusted aids: Jyotish, Tom Dunks and Tom Hopkins. Between them, he felt, whatever came up could be successfully managed.

The Farm was officially opened on 4 July 1969 and on that same day the influx began. People began literally to flock in; it was not unusual to see several cars waiting in line at the entrance driveway. In the words of Jyotish, "Most of them knew nothing whatever about Yoga, swamiji (Kriyananda), or Master's teachings. Many of them were drug-oriented hippies who wanted to go back to the land, but not to any kind of work. They weren't concerned with the mortgage payments—God would provide.

"Many others came for a variety of different reasons. However, to join the community they had to give a positive reason, not just say, 'I've had it out there.' Those who felt that way were allowed a visit, but were not invited to join. The were not bad people: they were often unrealistic, unduly romantic, and certainly not yogis, but within their own framework in each case they were trying to do something they saw as right for them."

Before the first resident set foot on Ananda, two firm rules had been established in advance, "No Drugs" and "No Alcohol." Within a short time Jyotish became known as "The Narc," a role he didn't particularly relish, but he was determined that the drug culture would not be tolerated at

Ananda. This strict prohibition was not generally known to many of the neighbors who lived in the surrounding area known as San Juan Ridge. Day after day they witnessed a steady procession of unsavory-looking, long-haired males with their women and a very understandable concern began to build up in their minds.

Many of the applicants for membership were much less visible and did not fit this description at all. Some of them were senior citizens looking for a fresh hope and, in some cases, finding it.

Very quickly the new community grew to fifty people. As Jyotish described it later, "The only thing necessary to join Ananda that summer was to say you were off drugs and chant *Aum* three times."

A high point of sorts occurred when one man drove in with a car, parked and asked to see the head man. When Jyotish responded, he said, "I heard about this place in Yellowstone, so I came here. I sold the furniture, the wife and kids are waiting, so where's the house?"

Miss Phyllis Offstein had been studying anthropology at the University of Wisconsin. Despite the fact that she had been raised rather strictly in the Jewish faith, she felt herself less and less attracted to it: she had not attended any services or religious meetings for some time. Instead she found herself drawn to the spiritual teachings of the East. The idea of meditation appealed to her, but after reading the first two or three lessons offered by the Self Realization Fellowship she realized that she would never learn that way. She would have to have a teacher. She was anxious to use her mind spiritually, but nothing in the college environment was able to stimulate her as she wished.

In her search she ran across and read *Autobiography of a Yogi*; shortly after that through a friend of a friend she heard about Ananda. After completing her studies and examinations, she didn't wait for the formal graduation ceremony, instead through the college bulletin board she got a ride to Los Angeles. From there she took a series of buses to

Nevada City. She had phoned ahead and was assured that someone would meet her.

Jyotish and Seva picked her up, took her to an auto parts store where she waited an hour, and then drove her to Ananda. Upon her arrival she found nothing material at all, which was a definite disappointment, but the people seemed to be wonderful. It was the Fourth of July, the first day that the Farm was open. As she sat on her suitcase, she wondered very much what was going to happen to her next. This was the place where she had hoped her spiritual potential was to be realized, but the beginning was not auspicious.

She went into the farmhouse to find out what to do; there she encountered a man in Bermuda shorts and the wildest Hawaiian shirt she had ever seen. He was enthusing that fried potatoes were to be served for supper. He turned and saw her standing there. "Hello," he said, "I'm Swami Kriyananda. You look like a Phi Beta Kappa."

When she recovered from her surprise at his appearance, she nodded. "Yes, I am," she said, and wondered how he had guessed. Later she was given a small tent to live in and a job helping to start a garden. She was not particularly comfortable with most of the other residents, but a girl named Fern Rosenberg became her friend.

It was not as she had hoped. The living conditions were minimal and her work in the garden was both unfamiliar and hard. For it she received no compensation, forcing her to live on her savings. Before long, thoughts of returning to Wisconsin began to come into her mind. The kind of spiritual living she was encountering was not up to expectations; only the Sunday services, conducted by Kriyananda, she found truly inspiring.

She was on her hands and knees, digging in the stubborn soil, when an older woman who was a member of the community stopped to speak to her. Her visitor understood that she was not used to the kind of work she was doing and seemed sympathetic. Then she volunteered a prediction: "You're going to marry Jyotish," she said and walked away.

To Phyllis Offstein that was preposterous. She had virtually decided to leave and while she knew Jyotish, nothing

remotely approaching affection had ever been generated
between them. She dug her hands back into the dirt and
wondered how much longer she would have the strength to
hang on.

Hardly a month had passed since the opening of the Farm
when a definite dichotomy began to develop between those who
were living at the Meditation Retreat and the new inhabitants
of the Farm proper. There were several different issues, but the
two principal ones were spiritual orientation and drugs.

The Farm residents were for the most part newcomers. Few
of them could qualify as disciples of Yogananda although as
Jyotish explained, "It would not be fair to say that those early
residents of the Farm were less spiritual than the people at the
Retreat. They were simply attuned in a different way. Many of
them literally hadn't found out as yet just where they were.
Those who had come out of the drug culture had a very different
set of ideas and standards."

This generous evaluation was not fully shared by many of
the residents of the Retreat who had found there the kind of
fully spiritual environment they had been seeking. While they
were meditating and attending classes in various aspects of
yogic life, some of the Farm residents were holding meetings to
decide whether or not Yogananda was really their guru, and if
so why. They also very seriously entertained the idea of trying
to sell the real estate on which they were living, presumably to
pocket the proceeds.

Also, despite the fact that they had firmly committed
themselves to the contrary, a number of the new Farm
residents were making steady use of drugs. This became the
subject of very serious contention between the drug users and
Ananda management as represented principally by Jyotish.
Clearly if this situation were to continue, Ananda as it had
been visualized, was doomed.

When some of the Farm residents began to discuss how
they might split off from the Ananda organization and set up a
different kind of community on their own, Kriyananda stepped
in. In the abundant joy of that first summer he was not anxious

to play the role of disciplinarian, but the need for a strong guiding hand was evident. He was aware that most of the people who had come to the Farm had done so with different expectations. Some of them were poor, others were badly upset. Often they had assumed that at Ananda everything would be free and that all things would be done for them, by God or someone. In a great many cases the idea of work was repugnant to them.

To those who wanted to secede he pointed out very plainly that there was no way they could do so. "You couldn't make the payments on the mortgage at the rate of two thousand a month," he told them. "So even if you took the land, you'd lose it and be off the property within six months."

It was through this meeting, and others to follow, that Ananda began to define itself. There was considerable traffic in and out of its gates that summer, and as fall approached certain things began to solidify, thanks in large part to the hard work of a growing core group that never faltered. Those who were simply looking for a more or less comfortable life in the country without too much effort on their part left. Those who could not, or would not, dispense with drugs also departed. One person who was discovered to be dealing in illegal narcotics was asked to go. Those who were sincere, and who were willing to do their part toward the fulfilling of the Ananda ideal, stayed.

In November of 1969, as winter was rapidly approaching, Kriyananda called a meeting of everyone at the Retreat. When all were assembled, he pointed out that two distinct groups had developed at the community: those who came to lead a life for God, and those who came for different, if wholly honorable, reasons. This latter group, he said, was not in tune with Ananda's direction. He then gave two choices: either the community would become one wholly dedicated to God and to Yogananda or he would leave.

From that point forward the direction of Ananda was reenforced and the will was generated to make it work. A number of the residents left the Retreat to find winter jobs in the city where they might make some money for the community. As the weather grew cooler, someone suggested the idea of teepees; reputedly they were easy to make and provided good shelter at minimum costs. Some of the male members went to work cutting and scraping poles while the women sewed covers without the benefit of either instructions or a pattern. Platforms were built and the teepees erected. They were far from ideal, but they did seem to work. At least they were better than some of the small tents that had been in use, and considerably better than sleeping outside, which many of the residents had been doing.

When the gardening season closed down Phyllis Offstein left to return to Wisconsin. Other members and prospective members also departed, but those who were already truly dedicated dug in and waited for the first snow to fall.

John Helin did not know it, but he was virtually predestined to become a resident of Ananda. For some time he had been considering a sort of hermitage, one consisting of a series of single dwellings where an assortment of craft activities could be carried out. One evening he went to a satsang at a friend's house and there he met Kriyananda. All told there were thirty five people at the meeting and all of them seemed to be interested in the new community being established in Nevada County.

John decided to try it out and signed up to attend some classes at the Retreat. He had not been at Ananda very long before he knew that he had found something in being that was better than the plans he had tentatively laid. There was very little in the way of actual facilities as yet, but he understood that they would come in time. He did, however, need to find something with which to support himself and possibly to bring a little additional revenue into the community.

He made his wishes known to Kriyananda and got an immediate response. "How would you like to take over the bean sprout business?" he was asked.

A going business was far more than Helin had anticipated; he agreed at once. He knew nothing whatever about bean sprouts or how they could be sold, but any reasonable money making business was most acceptable to him.

With considerable interest he went with the swami to the temple. Underneath it there was a hopeless-appearing jumble of broken plywood, motors and miscellaneous equipment. On his hands and knees Helin hauled it all out. None of it appeared to make any sense at all and much of what was actually there was broken.

"That's the bean sprout business," the swami said. "I paid twenty five hundred dollars for it. One of our lady members wanted it very badly, but I'm afraid she ran it into the ground."

Helen did his best for the next two or three days, but the pile of obvious junk refused to reveal itself as being of any value at all. Certainly it gave no clue to the care and feeding of bean sprouts. Today at Ananda when something of a totally hopeless nature appears, it is automatically referred to as a bean sprout business.

Some of those who came to Ananda that first year were young people, others were not. Haanel Cassidy already enjoyed senior citizen status when he arrived at the Meditation Retreat. Having received Kriya initiation many years before, he had chosen the yogic community as the place where he wanted to live out his retirement. Neither he nor anyone else foresaw the major impact he was to have on the whole welfare and progress of Ananda.

When the rains came and the cold weather, those who were still at the Farm or at the Meditation Retreat burrowed in as best they could. Conditions deteriorated from the barely acceptable to the severe. There was little heat, no flush toilets and very limited amenities of any kind. Kriyananda was away most of the time, giving lectures and classes to raise the necessary money to meet the mortgage payments.

One condition of the purchase of the Farm was that the sellers would put in satisfactory roads for the use of the future residents. When they failed to do so, the swami withheld payment until they performed under the contract. It was a good thing he had the excuse, for funds were running very low and the welcome income from the summer classes at the Retreat was long gone.

He got no sympathy from the sellers: on 15 March he was notified that if he didn't pay $4,500 past due, plus the regular $2000 monthly installment, they would foreclose. He managed to get them to extend the deadline to June 1st and then opened some new classes in Sacramento to try and raise the additional funds. Only six students enrolled.

As the fatal date approached it seemed increasingly clear that the payment could not possibly be met. John Preston, one of the residents, had started a small business making incense and enclosing flowers in small cubes of plastic. He sold his products on the streets in San Francisco to try and help with the payments, but his contribution was not nearly enough to have a significant impact.

But someone must have been in the temple chanting "Aum, Guru; Aum, Guru...." and it is difficult not to believe that on some higher plane Yogananda had been listening. The unadorned fact is that at the very last moment a completely unexpected donation of $1,500 was received to be used in whatever manner the community desired. Kriyananda paid the bill in full on May 30th.

The first, and the worst, winter was over. The air softened and a few growing things began to turn green. At that time some of the faithful who had earned the honor received their spiritual names. There was a purpose behind it. Western names do not commonly have a spiritual significance, Sanskrit names do. And the bestowing of a new name signified a full union with the growing Ananda family.

For business reasons a non-profit religious corporation called the Yoga Fellowship had been set up in 1968. From the first, membership was reserved for the true core personnel whose dependability had been firmly established. As full members Kriyananda installed Sonia Wiberg as Seva, John Novak as Jyotish, John Preston as Binay (humility), John Helin as Jaya (victory) and a few others.

The dope-using hippies were long gone. Some very good people who had found out that primitive community life was not for them had left as well. But the base group was still strong and sturdy. As spring began to bless the land, Kriyananda delegated a good measure of authority and responsibility to each of his dependable people. Jyotish became the general manager of Ananda, a post he was to hold with distinction for the next ten years.

The domes of the Retreat were still standing and with the coming of warmer weather, classes would be able to resume and produce some desperately needed income. Already the fledgling community, by living out the winter, had beaten the strong odds against its survival and overcome a potentially dangerous split in its ranks. Through a series of near financial miracles, most of its bills were current.

As soon as there was a place for her to live, Seva moved to Ananda permanently and became the financial manager. It was duly noted by Kriyananda that she came to work every morning punctually at nine, setting a sound example for the whole community.

The swami had reason to feel contented, for he had up to that point seen his dream come true. As he walked about the Farm he had many thoughts of his guru and of all of the new disciples gathered in his name who had never known him in life. Disciples who were there to dedicate their lives to God through Yogananda's teachings.

Kriyananda paused to inspect the garden. He had high hopes for it despite having learned that the soil throughout the entire Farm was bad and that the section chosen for the garden was the very worst. Down on her knees, digging in the soil was Phyllis Offstein.

"You're back!" Kriyananda exclaimed.

She paused and wiped a tired arm across her brow. "I went back to Wisconsin," she explained, "but nothing would work out for me. Then I just happened to pick up a copy of the San Francisco *Examiner* and there, staring at me, was a long article about Ananda. Then I knew this was my home."

By that time out of necessity Ananda had established a resident membership fee. Phyllis did not have the money, but she had been accepted back on the basis of her promise to pay. When a job opened up in an old people's home, she announced that she was taking it in order to earn her membership fee.

That afternoon Jyotish told her that the swami didn't want her to take the job. She was to stay on at Ananda; Kriyananda considered her already to be a member and the fee had been waived.

While she was seated in a restaurant with the swami and some others, he turned to her and said, "I'm going to give you the name Devi. It means 'Shining One'."

The choice made her radiantly happy, particularly since she had never liked the name Phyllis from her early childhood. She knew then that she was truly and permanently a member of the Ananda family. It would be her life and her career. "Devi," she repeated to herself, "Devi."

And it was as Devi that she walked up the aisle in the temple in her wedding dress six years later and became the bride of John Jyotish Novak.

Things were looking not too bad that spring of 1970. But the few stout souls who were the essence of Ananda knew that it was only the beginning. Directly ahead there was an awesome mountain of work and development that somehow would have to be done. The question then was whether or not the relatively few willing hands available would be able to meet the challenge. They did not then know that it was to be far greater than any one of them could foresee.

Chapter Seven

The Tree Planters—Shivani

By the time that spring had come to northern California in the year 1970 Ananda emerged from a kind of hibernation with some incidental nightmares behind it. Its newness had worn off and it was no longer advertised on the grapevine as a possible place "Where it's at." The great influx was over and almost all of those who had been part of it were gone. Both at the Retreat and at the Farm it had become a true spiritual community built on yogic philosophy, and it intended to stay that way.

During its first year many lessons had been learned, one of the harshest being that the community had acquired substantial financial commitments that would have to be met. It was unrealistic to expect that Kriyananda alone would be able to earn enough to keep the sheriff from the door; other sources of revenue would have to be developed and utilized as soon as possible. One of the first actions was to establish a membership fee, both as a source of much needed funds and also to sort out the determined applicants from the merely curious or those only interested in giving the community a try.

The fees were set at $1,000 for a single person, $1,500 for a married couple or family. From the first, considerable leeway was built into this requirement. Those who were obviously desirable recruits were given as much time as they needed to meet their fee payments. In some cases those who were hard pressed for funds were allowed to work out their obligation. Occasionally applicants would leave the community, go out and earn the money, and then come back. In a few instances the fees were waived altogether. A degree of judgment was exercised in each case, a situation that continues to the present day.

According to Devi Novak, at that time Kriyananda was "a glowing energy of joy. He showed very little of it on the outside, but inwardly he was totally dedicated to God. He avoided any display of outer power." Unquestionably it was his frequent presence that supplied the necessary motivation and direction for Ananda. On the spiritual side, the secret technique of Kriya Yoga was a cementing element that bonded everyone together. Many of the residents had already been initiated; the others were looking forward and working toward the day when they too would be received through the sacred ceremony.

An interesting element was added when the swami, on an introspective occasion, remarked that the members of Ananda had been together before, either in their previous lives or on an astral one. The family feeling became very strong so that sometimes tremendous hardships seemed not so bad after all.

Although it was strictly a one-way arrangement, certain specific ties were maintained with the Self Realization Fellowship. The members of Ananda are also members of the Fellowship; it is a requirement. In order to receive Kriya initiation at Ananda the applicant, among other things, has to be a student of the SRF lessons. To obtain them, membership is necessary.

Kriyananda has explained this one-sided relationship quite simply. "It takes two to make a separation. They can put me out, but I don't have to leave. I have never left."

The Self Realization Fellowship, for unstated reasons, declines to give any figures concerning its membership, but in the year 1981 it was very possible that Ananda represented the largest congregation of SRF members anywhere in the world.

Slowly and carefully Ananda once more began to grow, this time from a much firmer foundation. Those who came to make it their home were for the most part truly potential "Ananda people." The new atmosphere that prevailed was very different; as Devi expressed it, "Joining Ananda was like a marriage; a commitment to a new life." The guidelines that Kriyananda had laid down were carefully followed;

membership had already become something difficult to obtain. But this did not deter those who were definitely sincere in their intentions.

Although Marsha Todd had just received her teaching credential from graduate school, and had a new job in prospect, she was not a happy young woman. She had been through a painful divorce that had left her a three bedroom home and a three year old son to support. Her energies were drained and she felt both inwardly and outwardly depleted.

At that point a friend came to her rescue. "I know a nice place in the forest where you can rest," she said. "Get a baby sitter and I'll take you there."

Marsha was not inclined to argue. "Take me anywhere you'd like," she said. Together they left Berkeley, California on Friday night and drove eastward toward the Sierra Mountains. Sometime after midnight the girl who was driving turned off onto a gravel road that was not very well maintained. After two or three miles the bare landscape changed to a forest; eventually the driver stopped before a small dome-shaped structure. No lights were showing anywhere. Marsha, understandably, was somewhat apprehensive.

When they walked into the building, a man who had been sleeping on a cot got up quickly, turned on the first kerosene lamp that Marsha had ever seen and offered his help. He reached for a form. "That'll be sixteen dollars for the weekend," he said.

Marsha was stricken as she turned to her friend. "You didn't tell me this was going to cost any money," she exclaimed. She had almost nothing in her purse. She was more than ready to turn back, but her friend wanted to stay.

"That's all right," the man said. "You can pay it whenever you want."

"Where am I?" Marsha asked.

"This is the Ananda Meditation Retreat," the man answered her. "I'm the retreat master. My name is Bill Cox, but here they call me Satya."

Too tired to do anything else Marsha took advantage of an offered sleeping bag and turned in under the stars. At least she was in a peaceful place and a rich quiet surrounded her.

She awoke in the morning to the sound of singing. She did not know it, but it was a very sacred time—Kriya day. When she went with her friend to the common dome for breakfast, she was greeted with smiles but nothing more; everyone was observing silence. Those who were to receive initiation were fasting. When she had eaten and left the silent dome, it was explained to her what Kriya was and that the day was therefore a very special one. She liked the Retreat a great deal, despite the fact that the rule of silence prevailed. At six o'clock she heard the gong sound four times and she saw those who had been chosen, dressed in white, filing into the temple.

In the morning it was very different. People spoke to her; the joy of the initiation was everywhere. After breakfast she attended a fire ceremony. When Kriyananda sang some mantras in Sanskrit, she followed his lips and, closing her eyes, sang with him in the language she had never before heard. And she found that she was crying.

She continued to cry during the Sunday morning service in the Temple of Leaves, an outdoor chapel full of the verdant presence of nature. She was moved at finding a picture of Jesus on the altar. When the service was over she went to the swami and asked, "Why am I crying?"

He only smiled at her, but in her mind a powerful and stunning thought took shape. "This is my home," she said, without thinking. "May I live here?"

"Is there anything holding you back?" Kriyananda asked.

"I owe some money on my car. And I have a contract to teach."

"Then you should go back and discharge those obligations. Do that first."

On Sunday evening she returned to Berkeley a different person. After meeting her teaching schedule, she spent her evenings studying and learning the yoga philosophy. She read Kriyananda's books. Each day that passed strengthened her conviction that she had found the life she wanted desperately to live.

When her contract had been completed, and her financial obligations met, she returned to Ananda to stay. Very quickly she became a member of the inner family, those who were completely dedicated to the community and its spiritual objectives. In the spring she was granted her own Kriya initiation and received the spiritual name Kalyani. When the monastic order was founded, she applied to become a nun, but there was the matter of her little son. She laid the question before Kriyananda who ruled that she could be both nun and mother at the same time, if that was her choice.

It was. Today a radiantly happy person, she is a teacher in the Ananda schools.

Bryan O'Hara had a slightly different experience. A San Francisco native, he heard about Ananda and went there to see what it was like. He went first to the Retreat, got out of his car, and looked around. In his own words, "It was one of those situations where you just walk onto the property and suddenly your heart just opens. You see people and all of them are just really honest individuals. They're smiling and they have bright eyes; you talk to them and there's a light in their eyes. That was unique; I'd never met a group of people like that."

He also noticed several signs that ended with the word *Shanti*. Obviously, Bryan concluded, Shanti was someone of importance at Ananda. Later he learned that *shanti* is the Sanskrit word for peace. It did not take him long to become an Ananda permanent resident; with genuine enthusiasm he built himself a home and then persuaded his mother to come and see it. Unfortunately while he was gone a raccoon broke in and disported itself heartily; when Bryan opened the door to show his mother his fine new home she saw instead something that looked like a minor disaster.

However, Bryan did not give up. There was to be a Thursday evening Satsang at Kriyananda's dome. Somewhat fervently hoping for a talk on devotion, or a similar subject, Bryan took his mother to meet and hear his teacher. When the people had all gathered and were ready to listen, the swami was in a mood to discourse on mystical matters. He lectured on the inner spine, the chakra gates within it and how they are related to the signs of the Zodiac. At which point Mrs. O'Hara rose to her feet. "Hogwash!" she declared.

Despite that unfortunate incident, she eventually followed in her son's footsteps and discovered the joys of meditation. Bryan O'Hara, meanwhile, as Santosh, had already become one of the Ananda dedicated core people.

On 1 June 1970, Kriyananda moved from the Bay Area to the Meditation Retreat and took up residence in the now firmly built dome that had been constructed for him. The total Ananda population had declined severely during the winter, but most of those who had left were not the kind of recruits and permanent members that the community was seeking. The schism that had separated the Meditation Retreat from The Farm was a thing of the past. Also, the word was firmly out on the grapevine that Ananda was not a place at which to enjoy both rural living and the questionable pleasures of narcotics. Its future as a spiritual entity had been well established. Then, on 3 July 1970, the temple burned down.

It was quickly decided that no one was to blame. The exact cause was never established, but the most probable explanation was that one or more candles had accidentally been left burning on the altar. Fortunately, the common dome, which stood immediately adjacent to the temple, was unharmed, as was the rest of the Retreat.

Kriyananda took this only moderate disaster as a sign that he was to build a larger and finer temple on the same site. Work began almost at once and was completed within a few weeks. The new temple was indeed larger and more comfortable. The Ananda residents, who by this time had learned quite a bit about domes, had no trouble at all in replacing their house of worship with a better one. It was solidly constructed and served the community as its principal spiritual focus until the World Brotherhood Center at The Farm was opened for regular services in 1981.

Gradually the membership began to grow once more. The

new fees deterred some, but those who were desirable applicants and who could not pay immediately were shown every consideration. The few old buildings on The Farm property were converted for community use; even an almost hopelessly decrepit barn was put into service. A great deal more urgently needed to be done, but the available finances were very limited since almost every dollar earned had to be set aside to meet the mortgage payments.

In order to earn additional revenue, a few businesses were set up, some of which were failures and some of which prospered. The flowers in plastic business was doing well financially when it had to be abandoned because the resin being used turned out to be poisonous and the people working with it became sick. A large berry patch at The Farm proved to be an unexpected blessing and provided some produce for market.

As the residents of the new community struggled to make ends meet, and to provide shelter for themselves against the coming winter, the family feeling began to grow. Already the Ananda population was made up of people from many different religious backgrounds, but they were all second generation disciples of Yogananda and in that common dedication they found a strong unity. When the winter did come they weathered it well. The Sunday services in the temple, usually led by Kriyananda, gave inspiration to all. In addition, the swami's presence provided, in the words of one resident, "A beacon of energy." He had sensed that his community was going to succeed where so many hundreds of others had failed. He continued to raise money for it with public appearances and classes, but the entire burden no longer rested on him alone. Meanwhile, elsewhere in the nation, things were happening that were to have a major impact on the future of Ananda.

Little Fern Rosenberg was born into an orthodox Jewish family, the only child of a pharmacist. At the age of six she was enrolled in Hebrew school where she took her religious training very seriously; for the next seven years she attended the classes given there four days a week after regular school, and on every Saturday. Each of her summers during this period she spent at religious camp. Since she was notably bright, her progress was substantial: by the time she was thirteen she was more than ready for her bar mitzvah—but she was not a male. There was a female equivalent, but this she refused. She had one great and consuming ambition which she was fully qualified by education to fulfill: she wanted to be called up during service to read from the Torah. She was perfectly aware that girls were not called for this purpose, but she proposed to become the first.

Despite her intensive and dedicated studies, tradition prevailed and she was never summoned. And despite her anguish at being refused, when she knew herself so well qualified to be called, she never, then or later, became a feminist.

She was denied but not defeated. In her mind a new determination took shape: she would go to law school.

This time she would not be denied. She enrolled in the George Washington Law School in 1966 with the full intention of practicing law for her career. However, the tough-minded little girl who had tried unsuccessfully to break the barrier to her sex and praise God by reading from the sacred book, found that she was too idealistic for a legal career.

In her words:

"I always wanted to learn to live rightly—how to be good and just. To learn to help other people. These were exactly the wrong reasons for going to law school. From the first day I was disillusioned. During the first meeting of my constitutional law class the professor said to us, 'There is no necessary relationship between legality and morality.' I was crushed."

In 1968 she left law school and set out to cross the country—on foot. In November she arrived in Menlo Park, California after having spent a full six months on her journey. She found a job with a lawyer, but she was still searching for something. What it might be, she didn't know. As she put it, "I needed a guru."

In February she discovered Kriyananda in Menlo Park

and signed up to attend his class in the yoga postures. During the next six weeks, while she strove to adjust her trim but small body into the required postures, she planned another cross country trip, this one through Canada. The first stop on this journey would be the recently announced Ananda retreat.

She went to Lake Tahoe and from there started out with her back pack and sleeping bag to try to thumb a ride to Nevada City. The first car that stopped had two girls in it. They were on their way to Ananda.

Later that afternoon, as the car made its way through the area that had been devastated a century before by hydraulic mining, Fern thought she must be on the moon, the landscape was so utterly stark. Then, when the trees began, everything changed. When they arrived at the small dome that served as the Retreat office, Fern was assigned a place to sleep near to the fire ceremony pit. It was her first home at Ananda.

Very early in the morning a gong rang, signaling the beginning of yoga exercises in the temple. They were led by the retreat master, Bill Cox, an older man who was both compassionate and highly adventuristic. Before coming to Ananda during its first season, he had at various times been a seaman, sky diver, and dance instructor. When the exercises were over he interviewed Fern and was impressed with her. She had very little money, but that was not a prime consideration at Ananda. He gave her a job working in the kitchen. That was 23 June, 1969.

At that time Fern had no particular attunement to Ananda's mission; instead she wondered what it was all about. The first week of her residency was a new experience in her life. But, inevitably, she planned to move on. Rather strangely she had two books with her, one of which was *Autobiography of a Yogi*. However, she hadn't read it and had no idea that it was in any way connected with Ananda. Then, unexpectedly, she encountered Kriyananda in the kitchen. "I think you've come to stay," he said.

She did stay and before many weeks had passed, she decided to learn to meditate. She chose a day on which Kriyananda would teach her and marched to his dome to receive instruction. She found the swami sick in bed with the flu, but since she had come, even without an appointment, he taught her anyway, giving her a full hour of personal help.

Throughout the following winter she remained at the Meditation Retreat. There were two or three small houses together with some tents and trailers. Fern lived under a tree. The city girl was one of the very few who stuck it out for the whole winter. She began to engage in spiritual practice of a new and different kind. She learned the postures and the technique of meditation. She also read and took long walks in the woods, in the snow.

When spring came she decided to do something she had never attempted before—work with plants. Haanel Cassidy offered to teach her organic gardening. It was still February when Cassidy had her report to him at 7:30 in the morning to learn to prune trees. He explained to her that it was necessary to see and understand the aura of a tree in order to prune it correctly, into the shape in which it was created. Apparently he could do it.

In the spring she moved to The Farm and took up residence in a teepee. All that summer she worked in the garden, learning a completely new skill and exulting in it. She knew then that she would never return to institutionalized life. Under Cassidy's direction, and with his help she and a few other garden workers made more than a hundred tons of compost, all by hand.

By this time she had found her complete dedication in the yogic path. This was recognized when she was given Kriya initiation and pledged the rest of her life to following the teachings of the gurus and practicing the Kriya technique. Thus it was that the orthodox Jewish girl who had thirsted so much to read from the Torah during service became a devotee of Jesus Christ, Lord Krishna, Mahavatar Babaji, and the other great teachers who preceded Yogananda.

In September of 1971 Kriyananda made an announcement that was to have a permanent impact on the future of Ananda. Some of the resident members had urged him to start a monastic order for the benefit of those who wanted to become renunciates and devote themselves even more sincerely to God. Since he was himself a monk, as his guru had been, Kriyananda agreed. He announced the establishment of an order to be known as the Friends of God, and set a time when those who felt that this was the path for them could come to the temple to receive their preliminary vows.

On that very significant day four men and three women presented themselves as candidates. In a moving ceremony they were admonished to devote the rest of their mortal lives to the service of God and mankind, foresaking marriage and accepting the restraints of obedience, poverty and chastity. From the small group of men John Stephen Blake stepped forward and made his commitment. When he had done so, he was given the spiritual name of Haridas and became the first of the new monastic order.

When the four men had all taken their vows, Seva came forward to become the first nun and after her, Fern Rosenberg. When it was her turn, Fern knelt and repeated the preliminary vows to attest to her devotion. To her Kriyananda gave the spiritual name of Shivani.

When winter came once more, the United States Forestry Service offered what could be a lucrative contract to plant trees. Ananda desperately needed an influx of funds and here was a possible chance to earn some hard cash. A crew of volunteers was organized to take on the job. One of those who offered to help was Fern and there was a need for two cooks.

In relatively high spirits a crew of ten men and two women left Ananda for a northern corner of California. They rode in an old bus that would serve as sleeping quarters for the men and pulled a trailer that would accommodate the two women while fulfilling its prime role as a kitchen. When they arrived the weather could hardly have been worse, but the location, high in the mountains, was magnificent. What the Ananda tree planters had not known was promptly told to them by the rangers: there was a starting time limit on the planting contract and they had arrived on the last possible day on which to begin work.

Far up one of the logging roads they set up their camp. The

two vehicles were parked in the form of a letter T for the greatest convenience under difficult circumstances. Then the rangers introduced the hoedad. This proved to be a sixteen pound tool which, if swung vigorously, would dig a suitable hole in the hard soil to receive a seedling.

Instructions having been given, the rangers withdrew and left the Ananda tree planters to themselves. Outside it was very cold and the rain came pelting down. The prospects were not very promising, but the vision of a mortgage eventually paid off hung before the eyes of the volunteers and for that they were ready to give their all.

The daily routine was established, one probably unmatched by any other crew that had ever taken on a similar job. The two women rose at four in the morning to start preparing breakfast. While waiting for water to heat and food to cook, they meditated. Because they were both kribabans, this was an absolute necessity. At five they woke the men; while they were meditating the women got the breakfast ready and on the table. There was no encouraging early morning aroma of frying bacon; in common with practically the entire population of Ananda, they were all vegetarians.

Outside the weather remained foul, but the spirits within the trailer and bus were high. After eating, the men picked up their heavy hoedads and set out to begin work. After the two women had put away the food and cleaned up the dishes, they prepared the lunch. With everything ready, they too set out to plant trees.

The old logging road up which they had to come had taken them into an area of steep defiles and awesome gorges. The pelting rain made the ground slippery, but Shivani took her supply of seedlings and set out to do her part of the job.

The area assigned to her was on the side of a very steep hill. The first time she looked down, her inborn dread of heights seized her and her knees shook, but she was there to plant trees and plant trees she would. She started to make her way very cautiously down the sixty degree slope, lost her footing and tumbled head over heels all the way to the bottom.

At that point others might have quit, but not the

determined girl who refused to accept defeat. Bruised and aching, she slowly climbed up again and gradually evolved a technique. She would hang on to a sapling or any convenient handhold while she selected a spot for planting. Then, balancing herself with great care, she would pick up the heavy hoedad, raise it over her head and then bring it down with all the force she could summon from her slender body. Soon the sixteen pounds of the tool felt like sixty, but she kept on. After helping to cook and serve lunch, she went back onto the slope, in the drenching rain, and with an inner mixture of courage, determination and sheer terror, she swung her hoedad and set more of the infant trees into the ground.

The crew was resting after a killing day when a ranger knocked abruptly on the door of the bus. "Move your vehicles, now!" he ordered. "You're under a big tree that's just about to fall!" Hastily the two vehicles were moved: seconds later the massive tree came crashing down onto the exact spot where they had been.

Very soon after that everyone turned in—after meditating, of course, and perhaps seeking spiritual consolation for sore and aching muscles. In the trailer, the dishes done and the things laid out for morning, the two women were tucked snug in their beds while visions of hoedads danced through their heads.

After several days, the very supportive rangers were back again. They had been maintaining daily contact with the tree planters and knew how much hard work was being done. "We ought to tell you," they said, "that the way the contract reads, if you don't finish the job within the specified time, you don't get paid. We can't help it; that's the way the contract was written."

After that they broke even grimmer news: the crew was clearly doing its best, and the quality of the work was excellent, but at the rate that the trees were being planted, there was no way the terms of the contract could be met. Even if everyone tried to work harder, the goal was still out of reach.

The planting crew held a hasty meeting and evaluated the situation. Then, there being no other sound alternative, they put in a call to Ananda.

The SOS was received and drew an immediate response. Almost at once vintage cars began to roll out of The Farm filled with Ananda people who had foresaken their regular jobs to respond to the emergency. Everyone who could possibly get away went, with the result that car after car made its way up the old logging road to the tree planting camp. The rangers offered help, advice and more hoedads. The fresh hands went to work with enthusiasm and by the hundreds the new trees went into the ground. On the last possible day the contract was completed—the work well done. On the way back to Ananda the workers, those who had started and those who had helped them to finish, joined in singing the spiritual chants of Yogananda.

A sizeable chunk of money had been earned to help pay off the mortgage and meet some of the other needs of the community. As for Shivani, nee Rosenberg, she returned to the garden that had become her first love.

A great deal had happened. The Ananda Dairy had been started and was beginning to deliver its products. The first community-owned business, Ananda Publications, had been set up. The monastery was established as *Ayodhya,* for the time being a collection of small individual teepees and trailers, with a miniature temple. A number of couples were married by Kriyananda in the temple and several babies were born to Ananda families.

Shivani took up residence in a teepee, firm in her decision to make the garden her life's work. When the winter came so did eighty inches of rain and she was forced to move. But her spirits remained undaunted. Ananda, she knew, was going places, but whether it prospered or not, it had become her life and the fulfillment of her dream. And when the Jewish high holidays came, the girl who had never been asked to read from the Torah conducted the traditional worship services in the temple. Many who were not Jewish, but who knew and loved her, came to the services just to support her in her time of happiness on that great occasion.

Chapter Eight

Rules, Regulations, and Nevada County

As the Ananda community began to show increasing signs of permanence, not all of its surrounding neighbors were overjoyed. Everyone in the vicinity knew about the cooperative village, but only relatively few had visited it or had had any extended contact with its membership. As a consequence a great many tales were told about it, some of them so fanciful as to be absurd. Ananda was reputedly a free love commune, a haven of drug addiction with many acres of marijuana under cultivation, and a colony of worshipers of unpleasant, multi-armed Hindi deities.

A certain opposition to the community began to grow, fostered principally by three specific things. The first was an ingrained distrust of almost any form of alternate life style. Few knew accurately what was going on at Ananda; many of those who did not feared the worst. The Nevada City area, in particular, was rich in history and tradition, and its people fought hard to keep this asset intact, even to continuing to light the streets with gas lamps. Being a center of tourist interest was worth a great deal to the merchants and business men of the little city, so that the very thought of the growing community so relatively close by was disturbing. Even though Ananda emphasized that it was a spiritual organization, *what kind* of a spiritual organization was not made entirely clear.

The second cause of opposition was the strong desire of many of the other residents of San Juan Ridge to maintain the rural atmosphere intact. They were automatically opposed to any form of development that might bring in more people, additional traffic, or a change in the manner of living. To them Ananda represented a threat that possibly could at any time upset the placidity of their lives.

The third cause of mistrust was plainly religious. Yoga was not a word that inspired confidence, and the strong attunement of Ananda to India did not enhance its image in Nevada City. Some very sincere people feared that within the Ananda temple false gods were being worshiped, and possibly in a disturbing manner.

Much of this was quite obviously based on a natural demur toward anything unknown or not clearly understood. At this time Ananda did not have any community relations program aimed at making itself better understood and for this lack it was destined to pay dearly. As long as they lived quietly and peacefully, the residents of Ananda felt, the good will of their neighbors would accrue automatically. Unfortunately, this did not always prove to be the case.

In one specific instance the community faced a problem: Richard Baker of the Bald Mountain Association continued to insist that the Meditation Retreat be relocated. Situated as it was on 67 acres of land (out of 72 that had originally been purchased), and operating very quietly out of the sight and sound of its neighbors, the Retreat did not see the immediate need to comply. It had become a very important part of Ananda and the classes given there in summer-time had already proven to be a significant source of needed revenue. Nevertheless, it was clear that the other members of the Association would never be satisfied until the principal activities of the Retreat were moved away.

By the year 1974 certain patterns concerning the community began to emerge. The drug-using hippies were long gone and they would not be returning. As of July of that year, 85% of the Ananda permanent adult residents had been to college. Also a high degree of stability had been established. Although the community was barely five years old, it had already been determined that the average tenure per resident would probably be more than ten years.

There was another fact that would have gladdened the heart of any industrial personnel manager: very few of the residents of the community ever had to be asked to leave. This evidence of careful selection has continued up to the present time. In the year 1980 four persons were requested to leave Ananda, the principal reason for the action being the use of unauthorized drugs. This represented a rate of rejection of less than one percent, a phenomenally low figure for any kind of human activity.

Some notable developments had taken place at The Farm. The most important of these was the construction of the 2500 square foot publications building, known locally at Ananda as Pubble. It is a rather striking structure designed by the versatile Kriyananda and features a unique roof that appears to reach upward in order to take wings. Unfortunately the design incorporated a double curve, somewhat in the shape of a saddle, that promised to be fiendish to construct. When the preliminary work had all been done, and the new structure stood ready to receive its roof, no one at Ananda, or anywhere else in the vicinity, had any idea how to attack that tricky double curvature. Work came to a standstill while the alternatives were pondered. One of them was obvious: to ask the swami to change his design. For several reasons that was relegated to being the last resort. An attempt to start the roof was made, but it was no go from the start.

A visitor to the community came driving up and looked at the project. "What are you trying to do?" he asked. Out of courtesy, he was shown the plans. "Believe it or not," the visitor said, "I'm probably the only man in the state who knows how to build a roof like that."

It was perfectly true; the visitor described the technique to be used and guided the start of the work. Today Pubble, with its flying roof, stands proudly on top of a low bluff, one of the most conspicuous buildings at Ananda.

By this time such convenient miracles were being accepted as a regular thing. Not long before the Pubble roof incident, Kriyananda had felt guided to go to India. He had been refused a visa for ten years on the continuing belief that he was a CIA agent. Finally he wrote to the home minister and secured the necessary permission.

Shortly before he was due to depart the swami's car broke down and $1100 of his travel funds had to be expended to get a new one. "Divine Mother," he prayed, "if you still want me to go to India, I'm afraid you'll have to reimburse me." That was on a Friday evening. The following Monday a letter was received from a complete stranger enclosing a thousand dollar check made out to Kriyananda personally. The letter simply said, "Please use this as Divine Mother wants you to." Kriyananda went to India.

Prior to 1974 a total of seventeen homes had been built at Ananda, a 900 foot square schoolhouse to provide elementary education for twelve of the community's children, and a small barn to house the dairy. The grounds were by no means crowded, but with the resident population up to 75 it was clear that if Ananda was to continue to grow, some additional land would be a very sound idea.

A generous piece of property next to Ananda had long been eyed as an ideal acquisition, but the owner, a Dr. Hoffman, was not interested in selling. It consisted of 326 acres with a farmhouse, a garage, and a few outbuildings. The idea of a new retreat had been formulating for some time; on the Hoffman property there was an almost ideal site that could be developed into the dreamed of World Brotherhood Center. Despite the lack of ready cash and the owner's firm decision not to sell, Ananda dared to pray.

Mrs. Nan Savage had come to Ananda on 1 June, 1971 with her husband. The marriage ran into difficulties and the two partners agreed to separate, she to become a nun in the newly-formed Friends of God while he became a disciple of the female Indian saint Anandamayi Ma. She worked for a year and a half as a manager and cook in the Retreat kitchen, then she undertook a variety of other jobs in the community including a four year stint as personal secretary to Kriyananda. By her own statement she did not consider herself a great success as a manager, but she possessed one rare gift— a strong empathy and understanding of the needs of others. Her dedication grew very strong and after proper training she became a member of the Ananda ministerial staff. To her Kriyananda gave the spiritual name of Asha. She is a rather small person, wears glasses, and is a great success as a teacher where her ability to communicate is highly valued.

Late in 1973 Asha was standing in line at the Nevada City Post Office with three people ahead of her. The man at the window asked the clerk, "Is there anyone here from Ananda?"

In reply the clerk pointed out the young woman behind him. The man asked her to step aside so that he could speak with her and she complied. Whatever his problem, she was prepared and ready to help.

"I'm Dr. Hoffman," the man said, "and I've changed my mind about selling my property that lies next to yours. Are you people still interested?"

Asha told him that Ananda was very much interested, but, honest person that she is, she felt compelled to add that as of that moment the community had no available free cash at all.

"That's all right," the doctor told her, "I'm prepared to give you terms you can live with."

Thus it was that in January 1974 Ananda through a lease purchase agreement acquired the 326 acres of the Hoffman property and thereby more than doubled the size of The Farm. Dr. Hoffman was regarded as a benefactor and never had a dentist been more popular. At once the tentative plans for the ambitious World Brotherhood Center and New Retreat were unrolled and a set of engineering drawings begun. The work went ahead with enthusiasm despite the fact that as of that time and place there seemed no way for the Center to become a reality. Even the first unit, to consist of a fine temple, a dining hall, kitchen and support facilities, realistically would cost nearly half a million dollars. However, Ananda was used to miracles.

It was not a miracle when the community heard officially from the Nevada County Planning Commission. The acquisition of so much new property, the Commission had decided, had moved the community out of the class of a church camp and into something else entirely. The Commission advised that Ananda would have to submit applications for zoning changes and use permits, as well as a complete Master Plan and Environmental Impact Report. It was then early 1974 and by reliable estimate, it would require up to six months for the needed documents to be prepared and processed. Meanwhile, pending their acceptance, a complete building moratorium was imposed upon the community. Not so much as an outhouse could be constructed until the entire process had been completed.

One of the things that staggered the community was the cost of preparing the necessary master plan and EIR. Hardly less disastrous was the building moratorium; housing was drastically short, with many of the permanent residents living in very small trailers or teepees pending available finances with which to construct better dwellings. Most of the homes that had been built were minimal in size, often they were about the size of an average two-car garage. This was partly due to the simple standards at Ananda, but much more so to the often drastic lack of finances. There was almost nothing whatever to spare and the moratorium forbad even bringing in trailers or campers since that would increase the number of accommodations available.

Ananda, however, had a secret weapon. His name was Sam Dardick; he was a neighbor, a yogi, a very close friend of Ananda, and he was a professional city planner with fourteen years experience. Work on the required master plan began in March with Dardick in charge of the operation. To help him the community assigned a draftsman, an artist, and a secretary-writer, all of whom were resident members. In addition to these full time helpers, many other members took an active hand in doing the job. Jaya, for example, took charge of an in-depth physical survey of Ananda and its immediate surrounding area and gathered all the needed data. Shiva prepared a report on fire protection; Chandra looked into police requirements. Other members prepared report sections on sewage disposal and the water supply system.

Within a matter of weeks all the necessary paper work was done including both the master plan and the Environmental Impact Report. Thanks to Sam Dardick the whole presentation was very professional and all the requirements appeared to have been met. A long-time resident of Nevada City, who has asked not to be identified, in a private interview stated that the Planning Commission was dumbfounded when the documents from Ananda were handed in. It had been the consensus of the members that the community would, in his words, "fall flat on its face," and that the requirements that had been imposed would effectively put it out of business. Instead the commissioners were faced with detailed plans and reports that were probably more comprehensive and better prepared than they had thought possible.

Then the nit-picking began. In particular the chairman of the Commission, Mrs. Sharon Boivin, seemed to go out of her way to find every possible fault and flaw. In justice to the Commission it should be mentioned that it had never been called upon to pass on a master plan and EIR of such comprehensive scope. The history of the community was supplied, a physical description of it was presented in detail, the geographical and social setting was covered, the planning process was set down fully, as were the goals and objectives. The master plan proposals were thoroughly broken down into six elements with many subdivisions under them, and the staged development planning was given in full. Then there was a summary and appendix with further data.

The Commission turned down the report and demanded another.

In due time a second full master plan was prepared. After months of frustrating delays and seemingly impossible additional requirements it too was rejected.

By this time the expected six months had dragged into two years and the necessary approval seemed more distant than ever. Ananda was not alone in its experience; others who came before the Commission ran into Mrs. Boivin and found her intractable. In its issue of 23 August, 1977 the respected newspaper serving the Nevada City/Grass Valley area, *The Union*, reported that two years previously the Nevada County Grand Jury had investigated Mrs. Boivin and had recommended her removal from office.

The Union reported:

SUPERVISORS FIRE PLANNING DIRECTOR

Nevada County supervisors this morning fired veteran
Planning Director Sharon Boivin, making public no reasons for
the dismissal but saying, 'the Board has decided to make a
change.'

The dismissal came after a 40 minutes closed door session,
with the Supervisors coming back before the public and press to
vote unanimously to oust Boivin. There was no public discussion
prior to the vote.

The 1974-75 Grand Jury called for her firing in its final report
and members of the panel criticized the Supervisors for not
following their advice.

At Ananda the housing situation had reached the crisis
level. The community was continuing to grow and the
moratorium forbad anything other than "temporary housing."
The law was so strict on this point, it was illegal for a
landowner to camp for more than two weeks on his own
property. In addition to Ananda, other petitioners before the
Nevada County Planning Commission found it almost
impossible to deal with that body, because in part, according to
the person previously quoted, of Mrs. Boivin who seemed
determined to block every kind of application of a
developmental nature. In her position as chairman she
exercised considerable power and influence.

When it seemed that Ananda's situation could not become
any worse, disaster struck from a new direction. A devastating
forest fire swept the community on June 28th, 1976, destroying
twenty-one of twenty-two residences and blacking 450 acres of
its property. A total of fifty-five people were left homeless.

In the face of this disaster Nevada County came to the
rescue. Food and clothing were offered in abundance, the
mortgage holders suggested a two-month moratorium, and
many other offers of assistance were given. The County
Building Department informed Ananda that permits would be
forthcoming immediately to replace the destroyed homes and
other structures, the moratorium notwithstanding. Then, in a
later action, the Board of Supervisors of the county passed a
motion that building permit fees be waived for the
reconstruction projects, a generous action that saved the
community approximately $1200 at a very critical time.

However, the money to rebuild was another thing. In addition to homes, the fire had also wiped out many of the cottage industries by which Ananda and its residents were supporting themselves. An emergency housing committee was set up to do the best it could. Every possible structure left in the community, including a tree house, was critically evaluated as possible temporary shelter. This process probably reached a landmark when, in the Village Council Meeting Minutes of 24 July, 1976 the following item appeared: "It was approved for Vasudeva to move into the goat shed."

By sheer determination, and much chanting in the temple, the community managed to hang on. More teepees were built since they qualified as temporary shelters. They offered very little in the way of living comfort, but they were better than nothing and they were accepted. The growth rate at Ananda was not spectacular, but it was steady and the membership committee had reports in almost every issue of the weekly internal newsletter.

Some of the residents left the community to find jobs and earn money with which to rebuild their homes. Much was made of the defects in the old housing and promises were exchanged that the new dwellings would be much superior. As funds were somehow assembled, new building began in accordance with the latest master plan and by the authority of the free building permits that had been issued. According to an Ananda resident who lived through it all, "The ashes were hardly cool before we were back on the land, laying out our plans for reconstruction. Never, at any time, did anyone suggest that we give up and quit. We all knew we were going to rebuild, the only questions were: 'when' and 'how'."

One more significant step was taken: a drawing of the first unit of the proposed World Brotherhood Retreat was displayed each Sunday in the temple and donations toward its construction were invited. The Ananda residents, most of whom had very little cash with which to work, dropped in their dollar bills. Some of the visitors who came to the services left a little more. Because of the excessive foot dragging and constant fault finding that seemed to characterize the

Planning Commission at that time, there was little or no hope of a building permit being issued in the foreseeable future, but the Ananda people continued to put their trust in God and guru.

Meanwhile, because it had been demanded of them, they prepared still another master plan for the community and engaged an outside firm, for a substantial fee, to prepare a new environmental impact report.

Another long time resident of Nevada County, who was thoroughly familiar with the circumstances, had this to say:

> There was no unified group in the Nevada County administration. There were quite a few who were against Ananda simply because they didn't want the life style of the county changed. They were afraid of Ananda and wanted to keep the whole area another Lake Wildwood [a residential development separated by several miles from Nevada City]. They quietly hindered and never helped. Some of the commissioners kept adding requirements. Ananda appealed for a public hearing and finally was granted one, but they were burned out ten days later. The head of the Planning Department admitted that Ananda's master plan could be approved in less than six months, but it was deliberately held up for five years.

Fortunately not all the officials of Nevada County shared this attitude. After the fire Mr. Jack Stewart was very helpful with suggestions as to proper drawings and other techniques that would give the Planning Commissioners no possible cause for complaint. He added that there had been a strong prejudice against Ananda's submissions because the members had done things themselves. They were not considered to be professionals as regards plans and drawings, despite the high quality of the proposals and reports they had submitted. Nevada County had started to grow at almost the same time as Ananda. Its officials had never had to cope with anything like the cooperative village and many of them were inherently against anything they considered unorthodox.

The general population of Nevada City was roughly divided into two camps over the matter of Ananda. Those who had met some of the village families and individual members were usually warm and cordial; those who had not were more susceptible to rumors and stories and did not want to know anyone who was in any way connected with the community.

While their third master plan was still stalled in the offices of the Planning Commission, Ananda filed for a use permit in order to be allowed to construct the new temple. Donations had been coming in earmarked for the project. Knowing by that time how long the Commission could take on any matter before it, the decision was made to apply for the permit immediately with the hope that by the time it was eventually granted there might be enough funds on hand to start construction. After all, they reasoned, how much objection could there be to the building of a new church?

On 23 August *The Union* reported that the Nevada County Board of Supervisors had voted to remove Mrs. Sharon Boivin from office. She was forced to step down as chairman of the planning commission, but remained with it in a lesser capacity. To quote *The Union* again, of 30 August, 1977:

FIRED PLANNING CHIEF GETS NEW JOB

Nevada County Planning Director Sharon Boivin—ousted from her job last week by a unanimous vote of the county Supervisors today was given permission to return to work as a lower level planner.

Also the position of Assistant Planning Director—held by Jim Louie—was abolished entirely with Louie to be retained as a Planner II, the same level as Boivin, if he so desires.

Mr. Louie, the planner assigned to the Ananda case, was alleged to have "sat" on the case for years. He was also reputedly implicated in the Grand Jury report.

On 8 September, 1977 the Nevada County Planning Commission refused a use permit to build the temple complex.

As far as Ananda was concerned, and most particularly its general manager, John Jyotish Novak, that was too much. The yoga philosophy taught brotherhood and the love of one's neighbors, but there had to be occasional exceptions. The community filed an appeal with the County Board of Supervisors. The Supervisors conducted a hearing and on

1 November voted in Ananda's favor. Use permit number U77-19 was issued allowing construction to begin on the World Brotherhood Center.

The master plan and other documents, however, remained as tightly bound up as before within the Planning Commission. Then, in 1978, the State of California put a new law on the books. It required that all master plans submitted throughout the state be processed within one year or approval would be automatically granted. At that time the Ananda master plan in its various versions had been stalled a full five years.

The Planning Commission had no choice but at last to call for a public hearing on the Ananda application. It was duly held. On 27 July, 1978 the Commission wrote to Ananda:

> After a public hearing under Nevada County Ordinance No. 500 and upon the evidence thereat submitted, the said Commission does hereby notify you that your application for use is granted, subject to the following conditions.

Almost a full three pages of involved conditions followed, but at long last the battle was over. The vote had been three to two for approval.

On 28 July, 1978 *The Union* headlined: "YEARS OF 'RED TAPE' FOR ANANDA ARE OVER."

The happy residents of the community could hardly believe it. The conditions imposed were both extensive and costly, but at least the master plan had been accepted and construction could begin. The community was still bound by the requirement that there be no more than one dwelling unit per five acres, and several new and expensive roads would have to be built, but at long last a day of greater freedom had dawned.

By that time Ananda was almost ten years old and despite the extreme hardships it had endured, it was firmly established to an almost unprecedented degree. It was ready then to look ahead to greater things and some very creative plans were formulated.

Chapter Nine

Fire!

Not wounded by weapons,
Not burned by fire,
Not dried by the wind,
Nor wetted by water:
Such is the Atman (soul).

The Bhagavad-Gita
Translated by Swami Prabhavananda and Christopher Isherwood

On 28 July, 1976, at approximately one in the afternoon of a scorching hot day a grader belonging to Nevada County was proceeding down a road west of Ananda. Because of a severe drought, the grass and weeds were tinder dry. The grader had a faulty spark arrestor; as the machine continued on its way, it ignited the brush by the side of the road. Within minutes, aided by a considerable wind, a raging fire was sending up flames and a thick pillar of smoke.

It was not until almost half an hour later that the fire bell began to ring at Ananda. Immediately everyone stopped work, put on fire clothes that consisted of cotton pants and long sleeved blue shirts and prepared to fight the blaze. The homemade Ananda fire engine came chugging up the hill onto Rajasi Ridge bringing more fire clothes and tools as well as a limited supply of water. Down below in the valley to the west, the fire was burning fiercely and was heading rapidly toward Ananda.

At first some of the residents were not sure that the alarm was real, but when the bell continued to ring, many rushed for their homes and to protect their children.

A decision was quickly made to try and stop the fire on the ridge, although the equipment with which to do that was

89

pitifully limited. Work began immediately in an attempt to dig a fire break, but it was almost at once clear that the effort would be futile. Fire fighting vehicles owned and operated by the United States Forestry Service began to arrive. In all thirty-one pieces of equipment and fifteen bulldozers responded to combat what was by then a full-fledged forest fire with many homes and other pieces of property in its path. During the next eight hours 442 fire fighters came on the scene, some of them from distances up to 300 miles.

Most unfortunately, there was a major fire raging in the redwoods and most of the aerial bombers used for borate dropping were engaged there. It was more than half an hour after the start of the San Juan Ridge fire that the first tanker arrived overhead. In addition, there were eleven other major fires in California on that same day, a fact that further reduced the amount of equipment and personnel available to respond to the blaze that was still gaining in intensity as it burned its way up the side of the valley.

On the far side of the ridge road there was a large meadow. A number of the Ananda men went down into this area with five gallon backpacks, hoping to soak the grass enough to retard the fire, but they were overwhelmed by the rapidly advancing smoke and flames and were forced to run for their lives.

Six tanker plans were diverted to the San Juan fire, but they arrive too late to stops its mad fury. When it came over the ridge, it was clear to everyone that the main area of Ananda lay directly in its path. Mercifully it was kept away from the Ayodhya area where the monastery and Kriyananda's home were located, but as it came down the hill onto The Farm proper, the many homes that had been built on the property were doomed.

Durga, a young mother at Ananda, rushed to her home with perhaps five minutes to save what she could of its contents. It was filled with heirlooms and furniture given her by her parents and grandparents, all of it beyond rescue. She had time only to grab few clothes and the precious objects on her home altar before she had to run out and save herself.

Minutes later her home and all its contents were ashes.

In the garden a number of workers were busy under the direction of Shivani. When they saw the fire coming, they asked at once what they should do.

Shivani, as has been noted, has an inner toughness that is not easily defeated. "Keep picking the peas," she directed. "There's going to be a lot of hungry people tonight."

John Novak rushed to his home knowing that it would be going up in flames very shortly. "I'm not attached to anything in this house," he told himself. "It's all God's property, not mine." At that moment Durga's young son came running in. "Get your clothes for goodness sake!" he yelled. He might have been even more explicit, but Ananda children did not swear.

If John Novak, a.k.a. Jyotish, showed less than his usual calm control, it might be attributed to the fact that only a few days before his wife Devi had given birth to their son.

As the professional firefighters swarmed over the property by the hundreds, those directing them gladly accepted the offer of help from the Ananda members. Everyone able to do so fought the fire desperately; there were constant small explosions as the propane tanks attached to the houses blew up one by one. By a very close call the publications building was saved and the fire was halted short of the old farmhouse that is now Master's Market.

All of the animals were released from the dairy: to a hoof they made a bee line for the garden where fresh growing vegetables awaited them.

By midnight the fire was under control and very nearly out. The damage was devastating, but that was not all: in making a too low pass in a successful attempt to save a neighbor's home, the pilot of one of the bomber planes had been killed.

Of the twenty-two homes at Ananda, twenty-one had been completely destroyed with their contents. More than fifty people had been left homeless, eighteen of whom were children.

During this time Kriyananda was in Hawaii working on his book, *The Path*. He had been feeling strangely uncomfortable all that day and could not discover the cause. A little after four in the afternoon Kalyani called him with the news. The swami dropped his work immediately and took the next plane back.

When he was at last free of his fire-fighting chores, an exhausted Jyotish went to see Devi who was in a safe place with her baby. "I've got good news," he said. "We don't have to worry about those leaks in the roof any more."

The fire had destroyed 996 acres of land, including 450 at Ananda. The property loss to the community was staggering, but among the membership no one had been hurt or injured in any way, and for that they gave grateful thanks. Several neighboring properties were either severely damaged or burned to the ground.

Unfortunately none of the destroyed homes at Ananda was covered by insurance, so the loss was total. This was not negligence; policies had been applied for and had been refused because the homes were in a wooded area. The Meditation Retreat, which is located at a considerable distance from The Farm, was undamaged and its facilities provided some temporary housing for many of the fire victims. Apart from the Retreat and Ayodhya, Ananda had been reduced almost to a bare earth condition.

The morning after the terrible fire, boxes began to appear on the streets of Nevada City, put there by local merchants to receive donations for the fire victims. Beginning early in the morning of that day cars began to arrive at Ananda bearing gifts of food and clothing. By noon the whole, large-sized lawn in front of the market was filled with gifts from other residents of the county who, unsolicited, had come to help. Many of the burned-out families and single individuals had been left with nothing but the clothes they had been wearing.

With profound gratitude, the residents of Ananda went through all the gift food and clothing, not so much to find what they wanted for themselves but what might solve a problem for someone else in the community. When everyone had been outfitted to meet their immediate needs more than a thousand pounds of clothing still remained; it was donated back to the county charities on the basis that Ananda had all that it needed.

An emergency fund for the fire victims was set up and reached a respectable figure. Only three Ananda families accepted any of the financial assistance; all three left the community shortly thereafter. Because Ayodha, the monastery area, had been spared, Kriyananda's dome was still standing. Many of the fire victims gathered there to plan their next move. They had lost everything, but they were determined to accept the loss and go on. Someone was considerate enough to brew up a quantity of tea, a beverage that is popular at Ananda.

Meanwhile the Red Cross, on the job as it always is when disaster strikes, arrived on the scene to give immediate help to those who had been left destitute. When the Red Cross workers were directed to Kriyananda's dome, they found those whom they had come to succor sitting calmly, in good spirits, drinking tea from china cups. The Red Cross workers were immediately invited to have some tea also.

Meanwhile two of the exhausted fire fighters from the Forestry Service had been kept up all night to guard a little 10 by 10 tarpaper shack of very limited value and containing nothing of importance. They had been told that it was Swami Kriyananda's home.

John Novak, who lived through the fire with his wife and infant son, offered some comments:

> When some of our people asked, "Why did it have to happen?" swami explained that it would help to explain the community's dedication to people on the outside. When they read about the loss of property they would not be too concerned, but when they understood that real people with families and children lost everything, but still went on—they might come to know the true spirit of Ananda.
>
> When it came to the distribution of food sent in by so many generous donors, everyone met in discussion. The question was not, "When do I get mine?" but "Who needs what?" People constantly said, "Take this, your need is greater than mine." Regarding the destroyed homes, people said, "Divine Mother changed the floorplan." It was not an abstract reference to God, but a very real feeling. Now the community could be rebuilt more in keeping with our true beliefs. Before people wanted privacy and

built their homes far apart, but now they wanted to be close together—they had found each other in a way they never had before. There was a real sense of God, a real spirituality among the members after the fire; I think this is important. We remembered when the temple burned down. Swami took his guitar, sat down and sang some songs of praise. When he was asked about it, he said, "I lost my temple, but not my voice."

On the day after the fire there was a community meeting in the temple at the Retreat. Kriyananda presided. The tape of the occasion is an inspiring thing to hear. The swami talked a little about God's will, about the tests that people are sometimes asked to undergo, and then turned his and everyone else's attention to the business of rebuilding. As some of the incidents that had happened came out, there was laughter. Plans were laid not only for the rebuilding, but also for raising the necessary funds.

There was some lumber on hand that had been ordered for the New Retreat; Kriyananda made an immediate decision to use it instead to rebuild housing. Domes were favorably discussed because they are practical, relatively easy to build, and fast to put up. Also dome building was an art that had been well learned at Ananda. A job bureau was set up on the spot to list everyone available for outside work and the skills they had to offer. A minimum rate of $3.00 per hour was established. A number of jobs had been offered in Nevada City to help the community and the trust fund to aid the fire victims was already substantial. The news was passed out that many local drug stores had contributed supplies of diapers; these were gratefully accepted. It was decided that the trees killed by the fire would be sold for lumber.

Help from the surrounding community continued to pour in. Ananda was given permission to dismantle an old flume once used for mining purposes; it contained a good quantity of still sound timber. The Red Cross supplied sleeping bags, household necessities, and work clothes. Lumber from an old ghost town was also donated. The mortgage holders offered a two-month moratorium on payments to help the community to recover. Whatever reservations some of the residents of

Nevada County may have had concerning the community, a forest fire was something that everyone understood.

All of this generosity was repaid by Ananda in an unexpected way. When the cause of the fire had been established, most of those who had been burned out successfully sued the county for damages. Although by far the greatest loss was at Ananda, Kriyananda made the decision that the community would not sue. "I didn't want to lay that burden on our fellow tax payers," he said later in explaining his reasons. No official recognition was taken of the fact that Ananda could undoubtedly have recovered a very substantial sum from the county, but there is no question that the community, and the swami, were respected for what he decided. Kriyananda's attitude was even more generous in view of the fact that Ananda was at that time in the midst of its master plan difficulties with the Planning Commission and was being given a very hard time by that particular body.

In the aftermath of the fire several things happened. Of the approximate 150 Ananda residents at the time of the fire, forty chose to leave, this group including the three families that had accepted financial aid from the relief fund. In the words of one of the core members of Ananda, "We could have told you ahead of time who would leave and who would stay. The physical part of Ananda was destroyed. Those to whom this was all of Ananda left. Those to whom the physical plant was incidental stayed on. The spirit of Ananda was left unchanged."

Kiryananda also spoke to this point. "The spirit of Ananda would not burn. When I returned from Hawaii the next day, I found spirits very high. It was a major turning point for the community, because we had reached the point where to grow further as a community demanded taking that further step of learning to think in terms of what is good for everybody, and what does God want, rather than, 'I'm here for my quiet little life in the country.' Those who weren't ready to take that step were holding back those who were willing. Those are the ones who left, and thereby made it possible for the rest to take that vital step."

Within a short time Ananda heard from a number of other

communities in the United States, spiritual and otherwise. As an example, the minutes of the council meeting of 23 September report that the 3HO ashram of San Francisco, a Yogi Bhajan organization, had called and had offered to bring twenty to thirty skilled workers, including carpenters, plumbers, construction workers and others, including carpenters, plumbers, construction workers and others, with their own tools for the weekend of October 23rd-24th to help with the rebuilding. This was only one of many offers received. Funds and physical help were offered generously by other communities and individuals. An experienced back hoe and cat driver offered his services free for a period of weeks. The community spirit had taken firm root and almost everyone connected with it and able to help did so.

The ashes were hardly cool on the ground before the reconstruction began. The Nevada County Building Department was of great help, as was the Board of Supervisors. Many individual merchants donated goods and offered jobs. Thanks to the emergency building permits that had been issued gratis, the ring of hammers on nails was heard throughout the grounds of Ananda. The master plan then before the Planning Commission was followed and through steady, increasing effort, the community rebuilt. Additional precautions against fire were taken, large water containers were installed near each new home, and the fallen trees were sold and hauled away.

What had once been a tree-covered lovely area stood as a large bare and open site, but the crisis, if there ever had been one, was over. New domes went up and these were waterproof. Not too much could be done, for funds were very scarce and while no one knew it at the time, the master plan approval process still had almost two more years to go. But the sun rose each morning and when it did, the Ananda people began their days in meditation, gathering strength, and with it carried on. They knew that a great deal lay ahead of them, and in that they were right.

Chapter Ten

Life at Ananda

It isn't that Ananda is a perfect place. No mere place, no matter how beautiful, could ever be. But for those of us who belong here, it is like a dream come true. It is a joyous state of mind.
An Ananda resident

The visitor who drives down Tyler Foote Road in search of Ananda will come first to an area with a long white fence where there is a short entrance driveway. This is part of the new land where the Apprentice Training Program is based. This unusual activity, which begins in early spring and lasts until late fall, is the point of entry to the cooperative village for many of its new members. Anyone who successfully goes through the Apprentice Program is very likely to be the kind of person who will like Ananda and who will be well liked in return.

The program has been defined by Ananda in its literature as "a working laboratory for developing 'how to live' skills." There are regular classes in both spiritual and practical subjects and working sessions in such things as carpentry, blacksmithing, gardening and animal husbandry. In addition, the apprentices, male and female, learn about cooperative living as they work and mingle with the regular members of the community. In the words of the brochure, "You'll learn how to spiritualize your daily life, your environment and your relationship with others, how to deal with moods and emotions, how to be joyful all the time."

The joy, in this instance, has to be earned. Here is a typical daily schedule for the Ananda apprentices:

5:A.M.   Wake up
5:15-5:45 Hatha yoga postures

97

5:45-6:15	Meditation
6:15-6:30	Energization exercises
6:30	Breakfast
7:30	Work (known at Ananda as karma yoga)
11:30	Stop work
12:00-1:30	Lunch and relaxation
1:30-4:30	Karma yoga
4:30-5:00	Clean up
5:00-6:00	Energization exercises and yoga posture
6:00-7:00	Meditation
7:00-8:00	Dinner and free time
8:00	Evening satsang and classes

Minimum stay: two months

To which the following footnote is added:

"Those who are accepted are expected to be on a spiritual path (though not necessarily our own) and to practice meditation."

A look at the above schedule suggests that they could hardly avoid it.

Here are some of the reasons apprentices have given for joining the program.

"I visited Ananda for the weekend. I wanted to learn a disciplined life, so far I've stayed two months....I love it here."

"My teacher advised me to come to Ananda to find out what I was seeking. When I reached here, I felt that I had come home. I had a spiritual family."

"I met someone from Ananda and came to the Retreat just for the weekend. Once I was here, I joined the Apprentice Program. What I've learned here I'm going to carry through the rest of my life."

"I had been planning to come to Ananda for some time. I had been reading the *Fourteen Steps*. Now I find that my energies are way up there."

"I came because of swami. He was so understandable—he spoke the language I could understand. He encourages you to develop your own intuition."

"I found that people have fun here. I have been here before, although this is actually my first visit. The spirit of joy is everywhere, people enjoying themselves in all situations."

These comments are from the enrollees who came, liked

what they found and stayed. Undoubtedly there were some who tried out the program, did not care for it and left.

The Apprentice Program is primarily designed for young people, although there are no age restrictions. The director is Prahlad, a very personable and gifted young man who is the scion of one of the best known families in the country. Since he has a very attractive personality, his social success was assured when, in 1973 at the age of twenty-two, he made the decision to forego it all in order to join the monastic order, the Friends of God, at Ananda. He relates to the apprentices very well, particularly since he is a deeply sympathetic person as well as an ordained Ananda minister. As a personal counselor he has a rare and remarkable ability. In his position it would be hard to imagine a better man.

More mature persons who come to Ananda are likely to go first to the Meditation Retreat, although there are always plenty of young people there as well. The Retreat offers shorter programs as well as the full Yoga Teachers' Training Course which requires a minimum of three months. Courses are offered throughout the year in Yoga, meditation, teacher training, biodynamic gardening and farming, and the art of joyful cooking. Weekend seminars are regularly offered in spiritual marriage and family life, methods of radiant health and well being, secret teachings of the Bible, and superconscious living.

This by no means exhausts the curriculum. The yoga teacher training intensive course (5 weeks) is very popular, as are the courses in joymatics, health awareness and nutrition (vegetarian), the joy of running, how to live education, and a special one week "Experience Ananda" apprenticeship.

Each Sunday there are services in the temple. Formerly the whole community came, but when the new temple at The Farm became available, the principal services were most often held there. Occasionally Kriyananda would conduct them; in the warm weather the Temple of the Leaves, a most agreeable outdoor setting, is used.

The Retreat is one of the principal sources of necessary income for the community. The enrollees seem to like it very much, for many of them return year after year to take additional courses. Normally there are twelve faculty members and a flexible number of guests. More can come if they are willing to camp out or use sleeping bags. The permanent guest facilities consist of five cabins that sleep two or three each, and small dorms. There is no indoor plumbing in any of the cabins, but it has been noted that when the roof leaks, there is running water.

There is a sign at the Meditation Retreat that fully expresses the spirit of the place. It reads: *Don't Believe You Can't.*

Some of the permanent Ananda residents came through the apprentice program, some through the Retreat, and some came directly in, almost always by previous arrangement. By no means are all of the applicants accepted. The requirements for permanent membership are clearly stated:

1. An applicant must be a disciple of Paramhansa Yogananda, and his line of gurus.

2. He must have studied, or be in the process of studying, the Self Realization Fellowship lessons and the *Fourteen Steps to Perfect Joy.*

3. He must have read Kriyananda's *Cooperative Communities —How to Start Them and why.*

4. He must be definitely and completely off hallucinogenic drugs and alcoholic beverages.

5. He must be able to pay his membership fee of $1,000 for a single individual, $1,500 for a couple or family and also have sufficient funds to provide himself with a residence.

6. He must be able to support himself by having his own income or by taking a job in one of the Ananda industries. (These are usually readily available.) State welfare support is not acceptable as a means of livelihood; Ananda wishes to be a self-sufficient community independent of outside support. It is recommended that married couples have approximately $3,000 saved above membership fees to cover the expenses involved in getting settled during the first year of residency.

As has been previously indicated, there is a good deal of flexibility in these requirements so that each applicant member or family can be individually treated. The decisions made are álmost always based on spiritual grounds; desirable applicants who cannot immediately meet the membership fees are shown every consideration.

When a new member or family moves in, provisional membership is granted for a period of several weeks or months in order to allow the community to evaluate the candidate and for him to decide how well he likes Ananda living. There is no fixed time for this probationary period; when the time is right and there is mutual agreement, full membership will come to vote.

In 1981 the permanent members of Ananda had come not only from the United States, but also from Canada, England, Holland, Germany, Switzerland, Italy, Bangladesh, and several other countries. Despite a considerable diversity of background, they form a spiritual family that ignores both religious and racial distinctions.

All resident members of Ananda pay rent for their quarters, but at rates that would appear as giveaways on the commercial market. In addition, even these low rates are very flexible and are adjusted to fit the circumstances of each tenant. A single man might pay $90 per month for his home while a working mother with small children might pay as little as $15, or nothing at all. Not even the most hardened cynic could claim that Ananda is primarily a money-making organization.

While spiritual values are preeminent within the community, much of the ordinary life style of the outside world is preserved. Put another way, the ideal of communal living is not overdone. People own their own property, work for wages or other income, live in private homes, and meet their bills at the end of the month. They abide by the prevailing laws and mores of the greater community that surrounds them to a notable degree. Since Ananda was established in 1969, the Sheriff's Department has had to respond to the community only two or three times, in every instance to deal with outsiders who had come onto the property.

To avoid allowing potential outside thieves to acquire bad

karma, Ananda maintains an effective guard program that is known as the *Sagacious Superconsciously Sensitive Sadhu Security System.* It works very well with most of the male members of the community taking turns on duty and in undergoing training for the job.

Distinctive titles are a specialty; a notable one is the *Ananda Oratorio and Mass Hysteria Society* which was organized late in 1980 to offer excerpts from Handel's *Messiah* and other Christmas music. Very often the community puts on programs in schools, hospitals and other places where entertainment is appreciated. A frequent participant in these events is the Ananda Singers, a group of five vocalists who practice together many hours each week and who are thoroughly professional in their performances.

On one occasion the singers were giving a concert at an old peoples' home in Nevada City. When it was over an elderly blind resident approached Ram, one of the singers who played linebacker for the San Francisco 49ers before he left professional sports to become an Ananda monk. "You from that bunch of kooks that lives out a ways?" he asked.

When Ram acknowledged that that was correct, the blind man offered his opinion. "Well, I gotta say that you're the nicest bunch of kooks I ever did meet."

Surprisingly, and regretted by some, the third and final rule at Ananda after the prohibition of drugs and alcohol is a ban on dogs. This does not mean that the community is hostile to man's best friend; in the past dogs have chased the deer that are part of the Ananda population, and such harassment cannot be allowed.

Even the inanimate residents of the community are heard from upon occasion. In the Village Council Minutes of 1 November, 1976 the following note was published:

> The garden has extensive fencing done around all its borders to keep out the marauding deer and cows. If you enter the garden, please make sure to close the gate when you leave. Thank you.
>
> The lettuce

Most of the housing at Ananda is minimal, although there

are many fine domes that are very comfortable. One of the nicest is occupied by Vimala, a lovely lady who bore her husband eight children before he divorced her for another woman. Unperturbed, she moved to Ananda with three of her youngest and became an important part of the community. She works for Ananda Publications, maintains an immaculate home, and is a delightful hostess. One of her recent problems was trying to discourage a houseguest from cultivating the taste of her twins, Luke and Sara, for malted milks. She would rather see them on a strict health food diet. Sara, who is eleven, makes excellent tofu salad which is sold at Master's Market.

Fortunately there is plenty of water at Ananda. The winter rains are captured and there are a number of springs all around the property. In downtown Ananda there is a fine new shower and sanitation building that is a welcome amenity at any time. Members of the community take turns in keeping it clean. In the atmosphere of Ananda there is no problem whatever with graffiti or carelessness in the use of the facilities. For a time trucks would stop on the road outside while their drivers hurried in to have a comforting shower. Regretfully this had to be discouraged when it was discovered that the uninvited guests were frequently leaving the place a mess. Also, it costs money to heat water.

There has never been a time when everything at the community worked perfectly, but there is an agreeable willingness on the part of the residents to put up with whatever inconvenience is necessary before repairs can be made. A full-time maintenance man is employed and he can call upon additional help whenever necessary.

There is a gas oven in the Publications Building that fell into disrepair and had to be taken out of service temporarily. A careful sign was put on the door: *Do not light; the oven will explode.* A free vegetarian lunch was offered to whoever would fix it.

There is a standard joke at Ananda which never fails to get a laugh. When something is carefully undertaken, and the result is an unmitigated disaster of major proportions, someone is sure to ask how it went. The usual answer is, "It was a learning experience." The implications behind the remark are always fully understood.

Housing at Ananda is a perpetual crisis situation. Three things are primarily responsible: the five year building moratorium, the devastating fire, and the lack of finances to build new homes when they were finally allowed. In order to avoid having the community classed as a subdivision, and thereby made subject to a whole phalanx of fresh rules and regulations, the decision was made in 1976 to have all the residences be the property of the Yoga Fellowship. This has worked out very well and as an almost friction-free arrangement; it has also made possible an extended game of musical houses which is played at the community every two weeks or so.

Whenever a property becomes vacant for any reason, the first priority goes to an expanding family that needs more room. When a baby is born, or a new family member comes to live at Ananda, improved accommodations are frequently desirable. The housing committee meets. Instead of just one family being designated to move into the new or vacated property, a half dozen or more tenants are all stepped up so that the benefit is spread as widely as possible. At the bottom of the stack a newcomer may be moved out of a tent into a teepee; the teepee resident is moved into a housing cluster, the cluster occupant gives up his room to move into a small home with his new wife and the former occupants of the home move into the larger residence where the expanding family will be more comfortable.

Since personal possessions are often limited at Ananda, because of the wish for "plain living," moving day is seldom traumatic. There are always plenty of candidates for karma yoga to lend a hand. Since the moratorium was at last lifted, the general style of Ananda homes has been much upgraded. Most of the homes lost in the fire were comfortable but small. The replacements being built are larger and have more creature comforts. At no time did the county impose size restrictions: finances were the principle culprit, particularly when the community was much younger.

The attitude of Ananda toward housing funds is well illustrated by a paragraph in the housing committee report for January 1978:

How can we raise the money? Well, it's obvious that *we* can't, but God can! In fact, He's already got it stashed away. All we have to do is to persuade Him to transfer some of the funds. By our willingness to do everything in our power, by our willingness to work together to build Ananda, and above all by our willingness to offer it all at Master's feet, we will attract the energy that we need.

Not many bankers would be favorably impressed by that approach, but the historical fact is that it has always worked for the community ever since the first piece of property was almost shoved under Kriyananda's nose. Whenever funds were urgently needed, they were always made available, one way or another.

Each issue of the weekly *Ananda Village Newsletter* contains a listing of the events being staged within the community during the following seven days, or longer. Here is a representative list chosen at random.

April 1 Bio dynamic gardening course 7-9 p.m.
          Housing meeting—Farm library—5 p.m.
April 2 Chanting/meditation—Cluster B, Jaya's house 8-9:30 p.m.
          Spring fashions at Mountain Song—fashion show and buffet, 4-8 p.m.
April 3 Walt Disney movie festival, North San Juan School 7 p.m.
April 4 Chanting/meditation, Helen's trailer 6-9 a.m.
          Gardening seminar, 9 a.m. to 4 p.m. Bring a lunch.
April 5 Children's service, 9 a.m.—Dr. Peter
(Sunday) Adult service 11 a.m.—Shivani
          Disney film festival, Yoga Fellowship Church, Nevada City, 4 p.m. and 7 p.m.
          The art of natural singing class, World Brotherhood Retreat 4-6 p.m.
April 6 Village Council meeting—Rajarsi Ridge school 4 p.m.
          Ananda Sacred Choir, World Brotherhood Retreat 5:30-7:30 p.m.
April 7 Healing Council meeting—Kent and Karen White's house 7:30 p.m.
          Noon meditation every weekday at the Farm Temple.

A significant part of the extra curricular life at Ananda is the continuing adult education program. Speakers and lecturers are brought in the year round for individual appearances or for courses of several days duration. The subjects offered cover a very wide range; they include music, writing, clothing design, choral singing, fire control, shiatsu (Japanese accupressure massage), painting, literature, mime, and many others. Representatives of other religious organizations are welcome. In this respect Ananda is exceptionally broadminded and undoubtedly profits from it.

There are two resident physicians at Ananda, Drs. Peter Van Houten M.D., and Deborah Way M.D., and several registered nurses. A medical clinic for the benefit of both the community and the nearby residents is in operation. There is also a clinic for other forms of healing including therapeutic massage.

The monastic order at Ananda, the Friends of God, presently includes thirty-three monks and sixteen nuns, all of whom have taken preliminary vows of celibacy, poverty and selfless service to others. They view the whole world as their family. Because they have no other ties, they gladly take on extra responsibilities of all kinds.

In most religious organizations the renunciates, once they enter holy orders, are provided for by their sponsoring church body. It is not so at Ananda. The monks and nuns are integrated fully into the rest of the community where they are paid for their services and in turn pay for their own support. Nitai, the chief monk, is the head of the Ananda schools and an ordained minister. Seva, the chief nun, is the general manager of Ananda. Many of the monks teach in the Ananda schools, one works in the print shop, one is on the faculty at the Retreat, another works in maintenance, and one in public relations for the community. They do not, as might have been the case in the Middle Ages, sit together in one place and illuminate manuscripts.

The monastics live at *Ayodhya,* (to pronounce it, say "The money *I owed ya*), an 18 1/2 acre parcel that is separated from The Farm by the corner of a forty acre parcel of land that the monks are presently trying to acquire in order to present it to the community. All the monks live in separate buildings, none of which are in any way plush. A proper monastery is certainly needed, but it has a low priority in view of the many other things that are even more pressing. There is also a Kali Lodge which is reserved for visitors and guests.

The monks and nuns rise at five for exercise, followed by an hour of chanting and prayers. There is a small temple at Ayodhya for their use. Any persons who would like to ask for healing prayers may write or phone the Friends of God. The number is (916) 265 5877.

There are no food facilities presently at Ayodhya and, according to Prahlad, many a peanut butter and jelly sandwich has done for breakfast. On formal occasions, such as Kriya Initiation, the Friends of God wear yellow; otherwise they customarily dress as does everyone else in the community. Each Saturday morning they join together for a five-hour meditation in their own temple.

In the past there have been instances of renunciates who tried out the life and decided that it was not for them. In all cases they were released from their vows, some to join the regular population of Ananda, some to marry, and some to leave Ananda altogether. The order is, however, remarkably stable; many of its members have stated that it is the only life for them. Keshava had long sought a spiritual environment when he was Michael Taylor. He found what he was seeking at Ananda where he is noted for his unfailing good disposition and capacity for long hours of work. He is at present private secretary to Kriyananda.

One young man came to join the order when he was only seventeen; he was sent back to college to prepare himself. He did and then returned to follow his calling. He works in the Ananda gardens. Another member of the order moved from his home town and college simply to get away from it all. When he arrived at Ananda he felt its blessings and the presence of Yogananda. He made his decision to become a monk and is now a very dedicated one who has never wanted to look back.

What has been said of the male monastics applies equally

well to the sisters of the order. Many of them are also teachers, artists and one of them works in the Mountain Song gift shop in Nevada City.

The question is bound to arise as to how a group of people gathered from all walks of life, and many different countries, are able to live together as a community with such remarkable success. The answer lies, according to Seva and many others, in personal transformation. The hunters who club baby seals to death for the sake of their infant pelts do not come to Ananda. Those who do, and for a variety of different reasons, find themselves in an environment where they are stimulated to become more spiritual in their own lives, to put a premium on harmonious living with others, and to adapt to the steadily improving life style of the community.

In so doing they acquire, perhaps by osmosis, the spirit of joy that pervades all of Ananda and those who have made it their home.

As Kriyananda has put it, "In years past when people wanted to give their lives to God, they had to enter a monastery. Few people are ready to that today, because nowadays it is very difficult to live for God. Very difficult to seek Him. They may spend their early mornings and evenings meditating, but there is usually a tremendous influence pulling them away. The world is so cynical; the world is so opposed to spiritual values that it doesn't even think in terms of 'What can I give,' but rather, 'What can I get.' Too often people think they are living a pretty spiritual life if they smile at babies occasionally, or give to the Red Cross. What I'm trying to do is to help start a wave where people will begin to see that if we get together with other devotees, we can create a spiritual world of our own. We want to offer an ashram to people in all walks of life, not only monks and nuns, so that everyone can serve God, children can be raised in the thought of God, old people can be happy and enjoy a meditative life with others and not have to go to old people's homes. That's the main thing to me."*

----

*From an interview with the author, 14 November, 1980.

The residents of Ananda spend a great deal of time improving their spiritual lives. They devote a lot of effort to the service of God. Otherwise they live very normal lives with, perhaps, a fuller number of real friendships than most. Also, indisputable, they have a lot of fun.

One visitor summed it up when she said, "The bloom has not worn off. These are not bright-eyed, bushy-tailed new converts, but people who have been through the mill and have still kept the joy they have found as fresh as the day it was born. You could call them 'The company of joyful saints.' "

Paramhansa Yogananda in the garden of his Encinitas Hermitage.

All pictures courtesy of Ananda

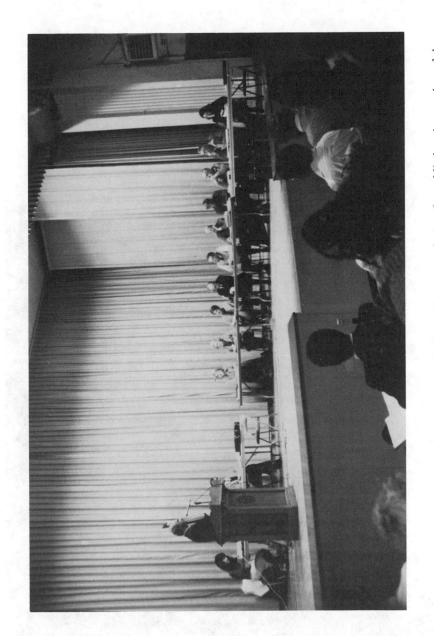

Kriyananda addresses the Local Agency Formation Committee during the public hearing on Ananda's application for municipal incorporation.

John Novak "Jyotish" teaching a class in yoga.

Haand Cassidy, founder of Ananda's Biodynomic Gardens with his main assistant, Shivani.

Marsha Fodd Deranja, "Kalyani"

Sonia Wilberg "Seva"

John Helin "Jaya" now Ananda's Planning Director.

John and Devi Novak.

Nursery school class in one of Ananda's three school buildings.

Self-Realization Fellowship Church in Hollywood, California where Kriyananda served as minister from 1955-58.

Early morning strawberry harvest for Ananda office workers.

A parent-children Sunday service in the Ananda World Brotherhood Temple.

Children learn about plants in the field as part of their curriculum.

Recess

Self-Realization Fellowship International Headquarters atop Mt. Washington in Los Angeles.

The geodesic dome is a popular style at Ananda. This is Kriyananda's dome with a stunning view of the Sierra foothills.

Ananda Reception Center on a winter day.

Ananda Meditation Retreat. Pictured are the temple, kitchen, and common domes.

Ananda kids in spring.

Michael Deranja, founder-principal of Ananda How-to-Love Schools.

"Downtown" Ananda.

A geodesic dome serves as an office at Ananda Meditation Retreat.

New houses under construction after the fire.

Yoga postures in the Retreat Temple.

Cleaning up after the fire.

Ananda World Brotherhood Retreat.

Overlooking Ananda gardens and dairy.

"Pubble" — office building designed by Kriyananda.

Kriyananda in India, 1960

Chapter Eleven

Yoga—The Path

From its inception Ananda has been dedicated to the ancient science of yoga. All of its resident adult members, and those affiliated with its various external centers, are yogis who have chosen to live in accordance with yogic principles and philosophy. In making this decision they subscribed to a number of noble objectives, the most important of which, by far, is the seeking of a closer relationship with God.

Upon coming to Ananda no one has been asked to forego his own personal religious convictions. What the community seeks to do is to intensify each devotee's spiritual life in the manner that yoga provides. The ultimate objective has been defined as Cosmic Consciousness, or an awareness that each individual is a child of God and as such enjoys a direct relationship with the Deity.

Yoga is a word that is well known to the general public, but very few are able to define it accurately. The most common conception is that it is a series of exercises, some of which are difficult of accomplishment, and which are designed to limber up the body. A yogi, in popular belief, is someone who is capable of sitting in the lotus position with the side of each foot resting on the opposite thigh.

Yoga is, in actuality, a religious science whose origins are lost in the ancient past. There is evidence to indicate that it was known, at least in part, as long as 5000 years ago. The word yoga literally means *union*, the devotee with the Divine, but in actual practice it covers almost as wide a scope as does the word *music*, and means as many different things.

The yoga scriptures are the *Yoga Sutras* of Patanjali which are most commonly dated circa 200 B.C. As in the case of

139

the Bible, many scholars believe that a number of different authors contributed to the project. The whole work is in four volumes devoted respectively to Psychic Power, the Practice of Yoga, Samadhi, and Kaivalya (liberation). There is some reason to believe that the final volume may have been added to the series as late as 500 A.D.

In the Sutras Patanjali laid down an eightfold path to salvation, something which should not be confused with the more widely known eightfold path of Buddhism. As aids to yoga Patanjali lists: *yama* (restraint), *niama* (the postures), *pranayama* (breath control), *pratyahara* (regulation of the senses), *dhyana* (concentration), *dharana* (meditation), and *samadhi* (Divine realization).

He also provided his commandments, ten in number. Under *yama,* or restraints, he lists five things to be avoided: they are violence, lying, stealing, sensuality and greed. On the positive side, or *niyama,* he calls for cleanliness, contentment, austerity, introspection and devotion to Almighty God.

These precepts, which might be called the ten commandments of yoga, bear a visible relationship to the Ten Commandments of the Bible. However, there are many yogis who cannot recite them, just as there are many Christians and Jews who would be hard put to recall the Ten Commandments correctly and in order. The modern day practice of yoga has its foundation in these precepts, but the emphasis has shifted to a somewhat simpler and more easily understood system of application.

A certain amount of yoga practice is physical, and it is this aspect of the science that is best known to the public. It is called *Hatha Yoga* and consists principally of a series of postures. The yoga postures are not, and should not be considered as, exercises in the same category as "pumping iron," doing sit-ups, or jogging. The purpose of the yoga postures is not to build up muscles or to increase physical stamina through hard exertion but to tone and condition the body, both internally and externally.

The yoga postures are called *asanas,* but the term is not in wide use. They are precisely what the word postures implies:

certain positions of the body which are assumed, held for a time, and then released. Some of them are very simple and can be done by almost anyone the first time they try. A few are extremely difficult and can only be mastered after a great deal of practice. The great majority of the postures fall across the whole spectrum in between. There is no established or required routine; each yoga is at liberty to select those postures he or she would like to do and they can be performed in any order. As the yogi progresses it is quite likely that some of the easier postures will be dropped as too simple while some new and harder ones will be added. When this is done, it is almost always found that the harder postures, or poses, are no longer nearly as difficult as they were.

Most of the postures are of ancient origin, and they work as well today as when they were first developed. Many of them have names, rather difficult ones in Sanskrit and very easy ones in English. Thus the pose known as *Halasana* becomes *The Plow* in English. Certain of the postures are considered basic, such as *Bhujangasana*, which in English is called *The Cobra*. Despite its jawbreaker name, it is easy to do.

A very pleasant aspect of doing yoga poses is the lack of sweat and strain that goes with so many conventional exercises. One of the strong guidelines given to every student of Hatha Yoga is never to strain to achieve an objective. If a certain pose lies beyond the student's skill, the idea is to give it a reasonable try, putting forth only enough effort to go as far as the student's physique will comfortably permit, and then stop. The next time it will be slightly easier, and so on, until one day, without any additional effort, the goal will be reached.

A second aspect of Hatha Yoga that is very rewarding is the steady visible progress that can be made. The first time that the student attempts The Plow pose, his toes may not come within three feet of the floor. But with each attempt it will become a little easier; the legs will, without strain, drop a little lower, until that electric day when the student, resting on his shoulder blades, bends his legs back over his head and feels his toes touch the floor. Also, when one pose has been achieved, it often unlocks the door to others that have been up to that time out of reach.

Some persons are able to do The Plow the first time that they try. Others may take weeks to work up to it, but it is a great reward when it comes. The value of the yoga postures was well expressed by Rev. Kanjitsu Iijima, the Japanese yoga master, who observed a student trying to bend forward to touch the floor with his forehead from a seated position with his legs stretched straight out and somewhat spread before him. The student was six inches short of his goal. "When you can touch," Iijima told him, "you will have added twenty years to your life."

To learn the yoga postures it is desirable, but not essential, to have a teacher. A good grounding is available in Krijananda's little book *Yoga Postures for Self Awareness*, which is available from Ananda Publications, 14618 Tyler Foote Road, Nevada City, California 95959. A more comprehensive and detailed instruction in the postures is included in his *Fourteen Steps to Perfect Joy*, a course of lessons that covers almost all pertinent aspects of yoga and which can be recommended without reservation. It should be noted that the technique of Kriya Yoga, which is available only through initiation, is not included.

There is a second physical aspect of modern day yoga that was added to the science by Paramhansa Yogananda. He developed a series of gentle exercises, thirty-eight in number, which are intended to recharge the body with energy, after sleep or whenever required. They are all very easy for almost anyone to do and the whole cycle hardly takes ten minutes to complete. If these simple exercises are done in the morning after rising, they do literally recharge the body with energy and inject a strong feeling of well being. They are a firm part of the daily routine at Ananda. The exercises are given in detail in lesson 8A of the first series supplied by the Self Realization Fellowship, 3880 San Rafael Avenue, Los Angeles, California 90005. To obtain them it is necessary to subscribe to the first lesson series, but much valuable information is given and the cost is deliberately kept low.

Probably the greatest single element of contemporary

yoga practice is meditation. This too is a word widely known to the general public, but there is a limited understanding of how it should be done. There are many teachers who offer instruction in various kinds and techniques of meditation, most of them valid. This ancient art has been practiced widely throughout the Orient for centuries and many different methods have evolved. Zen meditation is highly respected, particularly in its native Japan. It also has many dedicated practitioners in this country and in Europe. At Ananda meditation is a very important part of the life style and it has a great deal to do with the joyful spirit that so much infuses the lives of the Ananda residents.

Yoga meditation, as it is practiced at Ananda and at the Self Realization Fellowship, is a powerful tool in developing inner calm, peace and spiritual growth. Properly done it will block out external influences and permit the mind to turn inward to quiet thoughts of self and God. When meditation is practiced regularly, it is capable of bringing about significant changes in personality. Persons who tend to be nervous and upset may discover in the peaceful calm of meditation a powerful aid in recovering and maintaining composure. Those who are already calm and introspective by nature normally find in meditation an enrichment of their outlook and enjoyment of life.

During meditation the stillness of mind often helps in reaching major decisions, in overcoming anguish and in taking from disturbing influences the power to penetrate the inner serenity of spirit.

The simple desire to meditate is helpful, but it is not in itself enough to reveal its real benefits. Meditation as it is taught at Ananda and at the Self Realization Fellowship, is acomplished through the use of three basic techniques.

The first of these is called *Hong Sau*. It is a very simple method and easy to do, but it is usually effective. Despite its elementary nature, it is constantly used by very advanced yogis. This technique of concentration is not in any way secret; it is widely known throughout India, as well as in China, Japan and many other places. Complete directions for using the Hong Sau method of meditation are available in at least two places: in lessons twenty-three and twenty-three-A of the first series published by the Self Realization Fellowship and in lesson nine in Kriyananda's *Fourteen Steps to Perfect Joy.* As a first venture into meditation, *Hong Sau* would probably represent an ideal point of entry. Personalized instruction in *Hong Sau* can be obtained at the Ananda Meditation Retreat throughout the year. An advance inquiry as to exact dates, and reservations, is suggested.

The second of the three basic techniques is called the *Aum.* It is somewhat more advanced than *Hong Sau* and produces a different result. It also takes a little more practice on the part of the average individual before it begins to "work." It too is an open technique which anyone may learn and practice as they choose. Ordinarily it probably would be better to learn the *Hong Sau* first before the *Aum* is undertaken.

Although the *Aum* technique is fundamental, it is not presently included in the *Fourteen Steps to Perfect Joy,* an omissin for which no clear reason is visible. This may well be corrected in the near future when the lesson series is again reprinted. On such occasions revisions are frequently made to clarify certain passages and otherwise amplify the material which each subscriber receives.

The *Aum* technique of concentration appears in The SRF lessons 29, 30 and 30A. Unfortunately these are in the second series which means that they will not be received by the student until eight or nine months after his initial subscription and first renewal. The lessons are not available except in order and then only at weekly intervals.

Fortunately there are other ways of obtaining the technique. The *Aum* is taught at the Ananda Meditation Retreat in the same manner as the *Hong Sau.* A much simpler way of obtaining it is through the tapes available from Ananda Recordings. At present there are tapes devoted to both the *Hong Sau* and the *Aum* from which the student may learn these methods of concentration. Unfortunately both tapes are taken from public lectures by Kriyananda and do not adhere strictly to the announced subject, although it is included. It is anticipated that these will be replaced by studio recordings to be made in the excellent facilities available at Ananda. When this has been done, then Kriyananda's personal instruction, via tape, should meet anyone's requirements. A note to Ananda Recordings will bring a current catalog and prices.

Ananda House, in San Francisco, has compiled a little booklet called *How to Meditate* that is filled with valuable information. In eighteen pages it gives instruction in meditation, the *Hong Sau* technique, the energization exercises, the yogic eight fold path, and the *Aum* technique. While it does not go into as much detail as the other sources cited, it is an excellent reference source and more than worth the modest price of one dollar. It is available from Ananda.

One of the most significant aspects of yoga meditation using these techniques is the potential for obtaining a response. To some this may be a difficult statement to accept, but literally thousands have experienced phenomena which have indicated to them that they have made a positive contact with something beyond normal encounters. Certain things, in particular, reoccur frequently to so many different individuals, it is difficult not to accept the evidence that they offer as valid. Self delusion is not an adequate explanation in view of the number of persons involved and their continuing agreement which extends back, literally, for centuries.

Meditation has much to do with the spiritual, or third eye. This is a very ancient concept which is referred to in the Bible. In Matthew 6:22 Jesus says, "The light of the body is the eye; if therefore thine eye be single, thy whole body shall be full of light." And in Revelation 22:4, it is stated, "And they shall see his face; and his name shall be in their foreheads."

The third or spiritual eye is described as being at the point between the eyebrows, although many have placed it slightly higher than that. It is a point of concentration and one spiritual pole of the body, the medulla oblongata, at the rear base of the skull, being the other. Almost all visions of whatever kind appear in the third eye. If this seems a little esoteric, there is a simple experiment that will demonstrate forehead. Look out of the window, or at any bright object for a few seconds and then close your eyes. It will help if the palms are rested against the face with the fleshy part opposite the thumb, fitted comfortable into the eye socket. After a few seconds the reversed image of the lighter object will appear in the center of the forehead.

Binocular vision is made possible because both eyes feed their impression through the optic nerves into the brain where they are combined into a single, three dimensional image. This is the location where the object in question is "seen" and where the after-image just mentioned is consequently located.

There is a technique called *Jyoti Mudra* which, if practiced, will help to show the spiritual eye, but it is not essential. (*Jyoti Mudra* is taught as part of the Kriya technique). It can also be accomplished through the *Hong Sau* method. When meditation reaches a certain point of depth and concentration through the use of *Hong Sau*, a bright spot of light will frequently appear in the center of a deep blue field. This, in turn, is surrounded by a golden ring. This is the spiritual eye and is depicted on the alter painting in the temple at Ananda.

Without entering into a discussion which does not properly belong here, the *Hong Sau* technique frequently produces certain visual phenomena which have been known to continue for some time. Occasionally spectacular results are attained. A further examination of this subject, and an explanation of why this occurs, will be found in the *Fourteen Steps to Perfect Joy* course and in the cited SRF lessons.

The *Aum* method of concentration may produce a similar result, but it is primarily intended to detect sounds in the inner ear. This is clarified in the SRF lessons devoted to the technique and also in the tapes under preparation at Ananda.

The third basic technique is the Kriya to which a separate chapter has been devoted.

In every home at Ananda there is a place for meditation. It may be a small room set aside for the purpose, an alcove, or just a corner equipped with a tiny altar and a suitable place to sit. Each day begins and ends with meditation. Since most of the adult Ananda members have received Kriya initiation, and are therefore kriyabans, this observance is compulsory. There are also noon meditations almost every day in the temple. In the Ananda schools the children are taught meditation and are quite visibly the better for it.

The desire to meditate in one way or another is quite universal although it is not always recognized as such. When people are harried or upset, it is common for them to say, "I don't want to talk about it right now," or perhaps, "Let me sit down and think about it for a while." The familiar tendency to postpone a decision is another sympton of the unconscious wish to meditate even if the person in question has never heard the word. Meditation is an integral part of yoga and no one can follow the yogic path without it.

Not far separated from meditation is Bhakti Yoga, the yoga of devotion. It is a very passive form of yoga in which the yogi offers himself in silence and patiently waits for a divine reply. There is no attempt to whip up a lather of devotional excitement, nor is there any need to do so. It represents the point at which the devotee, after perhaps strenuous work and prayer, reaches a point in his development where a deep inner calmness takes over. "Bhakti yoga," Kriyananda says, "must lead from personal fervor to impersonal calmness. The important thing is not how one defines God, but how one approaches Him. The Bhakti Yogi thinks of God first in personal human terms, as Father, Mother, Friend or Beloved. Such a personal view helps him to awaken and direct love towards God."

Bhakti Yoga, according to Kriyananda, is essential to some extent for every follower of the yogic teachings.

Karma Yoga is the yoga of action, and of work. To quote Kriyananda again, "Karma yoga does not necessarily consist of building hospitals or doing works that people commonly label 'religious.' Since freedom is the goal, it is also the criterion of right action. If, for example, one's own nature impels him to work in the soil, gardening may be a more important—because liberating—action for him than preaching to multitudes." And later, "The true karma yogi tries, by God reminding activities, to redirect all the wrong impulses of his heart into wholesome channels." Emphasis is placed on the fact that the spirit in which the karma yogi serves is more important than the service itself.

At one time, at Ananda, by some mischance a considerable quantity of debris was spilled onto one of the principal roadways. A meeting was being held at the time. Someone who needed help did not go there and ask for volunteers; he simply inquired if anyone was interested in Karma Yoga. There was a prompt and more than adequate response. Working in the Ananda gardens is regarded as Karma Yoga since it is in God's service.

Jnana Yoga is the yoga of wisdom. Basically it consists of meeting the need to rise above personal likes and dislikes and of separating one's self from constant considerations of ego. It is the philosopher's path as he searches within himself to find ever deeper levels of realization of who and what he is. One of the basic goals of the Jnana yogi is to avoid the entrapment of illusion.

Raja Yoga is an all-over form to describe the yogi who tries to develop all sides of his being and in so doing make at least partial use of each of the sections just described. As Kriyananda defines him, "The Raja Yogi, or kingly yogi, therefore, is enjoined to rule his inner kingdom wisely and with moderation, developing all aspects of his nature in a balanced, integrated way."

He then sums up all of this in these words, "Yoga is the neturalization of ego-directed feelings, because once these become stilled the yogi realizes that he is, and that he has always been, one with the Infinite—that his awareness of this reality was limited only by his infatuation with limitation."

Since its whole purpose is the search for God, and since it provides its own pathway to that goal, yoga is a religion. It is singularly free of doctrine and ritual, which is a feature that has attracted many people from other, more conventional and traditionally western forms of worship. Many persons who have chosen to come onto the yogic path have mentined their disaffection with the relatively long and unchanging rituals which constitute so much of most Christian services, both Catholic and Protestant.

It should be noted here that the Self Realization Fellowship was named by its founder, Paramhansa Yogananda, "The Church of All Religions." By its nature yoga is very tolerant of other forms of worship. Services of many different kinds have been conducted at Ananda and all of them have been welcome with the exception of a Hara Krishna group that put on an intensive campaign to convert the community to its beliefs. The Krishnas were not asked to return.

The services conducted at Ananda are simple and basically inviting. They consist of a few monophonic hymns which, because of their nature, are called chants, some brief intervals for meditation, usually some further singing by the quintet known as the Ananda Singers, a discourse presented in a quiet, sincere manner, and a brief concluding prayer that asks for the guidance and blessings of "the saints and sages of all religions."

The tenets of yoga are drawn from the East rather than the West. The first and most important of these is reincarnation. As in Buddhism and many other faiths, the individual soul is believed to be reborn time and time again until it finally achieves freedom from this cycle and returns in a state of eternal bliss to the Infinite. This is the goal, the ultimate objective that marks the triumphant end of the Path. God and guru will guide and help, lending strength and mercy along the way, but the individual must work out his own salvation with their aid. If he fails to do so within one lifetime he will be reborn and continue his progress until he finally earns his freedom.

There is a yoga story told about the first man created by the Almighty. Since he was what would be called today an experimental model, he was made far too intelligent. As soon as he realized his situation, he sat down, meditated, and merged himself back into the Infinite. The next man created was given only enough brains to make his way and no more. From him present humanity has descended.

The second major yogic belief is karma, the balance sheet that accompanies every soul from incarnation to incarnation until he finally achieves a high enough level on the positive side to win his freedom. As a very general rule of thumb, karma is widely accepted in the East while it is, at least officially, rejected in the West. Nevertheless, the word is in common use in basically Christian lands and people speak quite freely about good and bad karma without necessarily relating the idea to their chosen religious practice. This is an interesting example of the extensive cultural interplay that has taken place as a result of immediate international communications and the development of long-range commercial jet aircraft.

A final point of belief is a major key to the understanding of yoga. It is the yogi's tenet that everything in creation is an illusion and an unreality except for God himself. Therefore it is a grave mistake to become attached to worldly possessions. This is closely paralleled by the Christian doctrine which advocates laying up treasures in Heaven rather than on earth where they will inevitably have to be left behind.

A discussion of these tenets will be found in the *Fourteen Steps to Perfect Joy*, one of Kriyananda's best writing accomplishments to date. Information concerning them will also be found in the SRF lessons.

There is a strong tendency on the part of dedicated yogis to be vegetarians. This is not a requirement, however, and many individuals have been medically advised against the practice. Most of the residents of Ananda are vegetarians by their own choice, but they make no objection when others choose to eat meat, even when common meals are served. To the great credit of the community, there is a wide tolerance toward matters of personal conviction as long as they remain within acceptable limits. Drug abuse, for example, does not meet this standard and is not condoned. At least one prominent and long-time Ananda resident was not a vegetarian and he enjoyed a glass of wine with his meals. Since he was a person who would never create a problem because of this mild indulgence, he was never criticized for this allowed infraction of the no-alcohol rule. This degree of flexibility has been of considerable assistance to Ananda in its continuing survival and growth.

These, then, are the principal elements of the yogic path. It, in turn, is the reason for the existence of Ananda and it provides the guidance that all of the community members have chosen to accept. It is not an easy thing for the kriyaban to rise at four thirty or five in the morning in order to have an hour free for meditation before the need to get breakfast and see the children off to school. But those who have found their path to God in this form of devotion do so gladly, seven days a week. They also attend *satsangs* and other spiritual events from which they draw renewed strength and dedication.

The people of Ananda, however, are not a group of grim and silent religious zealots. They are, as a whole, astonishingly happy and joyful. This is something that the visitor cannot fail to experience every time he or she sets foot on Ananda property or meets a group of Ananda members under almost any circumstances. In this they have proved their spiritual achievement and their realization of something to which many aspire and never accomplish. For, as Kriyananda has put it, "The purpose of yoga... is to open the windows of the mind, and to awaken every cell of the body and brain to reflect and magnify the energy that comes to it from the surrounding universe."

Chapter Twelve

Not Dirt, But Soil—the Gardener

"Now look," the gardener said, "and pay attention to what I'm telling you."

Standing in the sun, his straw hat perched on his head, he reached down and scooped up a handful for his pupils to see. "This isn't dirt," he declared, "and don't think of it as dirt. It's soil. Dirt is useless; it's something you have to clear out of your houses. But *soil*—soil will grow things, and give them life. God knows what's going to happen to this planet in future years, but the signs aren't good. You all know what's going on and if it continues where we'll all be. But here we have soil. It's very bad soil, but it still can be made to yield—you see that all around you."

He waved his arm to encompass the Ananda gardens that were his major interest and current purpose in life. "Even with this kind of soil you can raise food—good, fresh clean food— and you can live on it forever if you have to. Remember that when everything else has gone to pot, soil is the thing that will keep you and all of us alive."

He had said the same thing before many times, but he was listened to with the greatest respect none the less. And in spite of the fact that in a growing community of dedicated vegetarians he was not one himself and had no intention of taking up that form of diet.

Haanel Cassidy was, in every respect of the word, an extraordinary man. He was born in Japan in 1903, the son of missionary parents. Very early in his life his family moved to Canada where he began his great interest in the power of the soil to make things grow. In a fertile valley he began, at age 4, to work with plants. As soon as he learned to write as a small

153

child, he began a notebook in which he kept track of his plantings.

When he was in high school his father passed away and the entire support of the family fell to him. Despite his youth he took on the responsibility without leaving school and, when the time came, he worked his way through college. Already he had developed a strong sense of self discipline that was to stay with him, and serve him, the rest of his life.

After graduation he married and moved back to Japan with his wife, where he lived for several years. Two children, a boy and a girl, were born to them before the outbreak of the war forced them to return to the United States where they settled in New York.

While in Japan he developed skill that was to support him for a number of years to come: he became a remarkable photographer. In New York he went to work at this profession and found himself very shortly in high demand. This happy turn of events was offset by the fact that his marriage was breaking up. His wife left and returned to Canada.

National magazines noted for their exceptional photography, such as *House and Garden, Vogue,* and many others engaged Cassidy to do work for them. Gifted with a born researcher's mind, he developed many new techniques which were quickly copied by others. In particular, he created a method for photographing silverware that was far superior to anything that had been done up to that time. Professionally he was thoroughly established and his future as a front-line photographer appeared unlimited.

In the 1950s his ever inquisitive mind learned of something new: the teachings of an Indian sage called Paramhansa Yogananda. He found the topic interesting enough to leave his work and fly to California to meet some of the people of the Self Realization Fellowship. In particular he was impressed with Dr. Lewis, formerly of Boston, who had had the unique honor of becoming Yogananda's first disciple in the New World.

Haanel Cassidy was not lacking in interests. In addition to photography he had become a skilled and effective writer; he contributed many published articles on such subjects as aesthetics and philosophy. He made a special study of calligraphy and became a teacher of that engaging subject. Nor was his social life neglected: he was an exceptional ballroom dancer and was called upon to teach that too. His grateful students dubbed him Cassidy the Waltz King and not frivolously. As if all this were not enough, he was an excellent singer; those who knew him best swore that his rendition of *Old Man River* was even better than the classical one by Paul Robeson.

While he continued to study organic gardening, which was his first love, he also applied himself to a study of SRF lessons and other materials bearing on the life and teachings of Yogananda. A year after his first visit to the Coast to seek out the Self Realization Fellowship he returned, this time to receive Kriya initiation from Dr. Lewis. Once that secret technique was in his possession, he began to reexamine his life and discovered that the considerable success and reputation that he had achieved did not provide the spiritual fulfillment that was growing, day by day, much more important to him.

As a result, he made a decision. As soon as his children were all the way through school and on their own, he would retire and become a hermit. He began by giving up all of his possessions except those which would be essential in his new life. He gave away many of his dazzling photographs and deliberately burned all the rest. He learned of a piece of isolated property in Chile where he would be able to return to the soil and grow things.

He arrived in Chile unable to speak the language, one of the few times that his great versatility did not come to the fore. He did not mind; he intended to lead a completely reclusive life, raising almost all of his own food and spending his time in study and meditation. When he saw the property he had bought, his heart sank: it was just the sort of thing that would be unloaded onto an unsuspecting person unable to see first hand what he was getting. The house, such as it was, was incredibly flimsy and leaked both water and icy air. No sooner had he moved in, determined to make the best of his bargain, than the weather turned horrible and stayed that way for months on end.

For a solid year he stuck it out, but at the end of that time he knew there was no peace to be found where he was. Although California was perhaps his last choice of a place to live, he moved with his few possessions to Vista where at least he would be able to visit some of the SRF centers and communicate with other kriyabans. On the one acre of land that his new property included he soon developed an extremely productive organic garden. When he was not working with the soil or meditating, he went to the SRF centers to attend the services.

In 1968 he met Kriyananda and learned about the yoga community to be. He was invited to become part of it and accepted at once. Almost as soon as the first people arrived at the Meditation Center to begin construction, Haanel Cassidy came in with his few possessions. From that time forward Ananda was his home. To some it was not easy to understand, because at that stage of his life Cassidy was a sophisticated man who impressed many as aloof. He had very high standards, among them the self-discipline that he imposed upon himself as he had always done. At that time Ananda was in its most primitive state. He spent his first winter living in a tent in the pouring rain. The next summer a small dome was built for him at the retreat and he moved in with much gratitude.

Even during the worst of the winter weather he had made up his mind to one thing: if there was to be a successful community where he was, it would have to have a garden. He also decided that it would be up to him to make it a reality. Not long after The Farm property was secured, he went there every day and started to develop his garden. It wasn't an easy task. The new members who were flocking in at that time had little interest in getting their hands dirty in the soil. They borrowed tools and didn't return them, or brought them back broken. The final major factor was the nature of the soil itself: the whole Farm was very poor in soil quality and the area that had been selected for the garden was the absolute worst.

But Cassidy, although nearly driven crazy by the lack of

effective cooperation, stuck it out. He was by nature a perfectionist and he was determined that the Ananda gardens were going to succeed. He made compost and brought in as much wood ash as he could scrape up within the community. He did have some help; Devi and Shivani became expert gardeners under his tutelage. Cassidy was a truly great teacher and he had unlimited patience with anyone who genuinely wanted to learn.

Few realized that he was basically a shy man and that his aloof attitude was his defense against possible rejection. He was almost literally starved for the same kind of human affection that he saw all around him; those who gave it to him found him an extremely loyal friend. And the garden prospered.

By the time the great purge had taken place, and Ananda had settled down to the serious business of being a spiritually oriented yogic community, Haanel Cassidy had reached retirement age and more. But no thought of quitting ever entered his head. The Ananda garden, despite its hostile soil, was responding to the expert care it was getting. Tons of compost were spaded into the ground and wood ashes were liberally used to improve its quality.

A girl named Anandi became one of the garden gopis, as they called themselves. She had come to Ananda as Margery Stern and like so many others she found it to be the end of her personal rainbow. A warm and attractive person, she gave her full friendship to the man so much older than herself and received a full measure back from him in return.

As the years passed, Haanel Cassidy became a very special person at Ananda. He was the dean of the membership, but he carried his years lightly and his remarkable energies were demonstrated in a dozen different ways. He proved to be, among all other things, an excellent raconteur. In the words of Anandi, he had an incredible knowledge of gardening. When he was urged to do so, he sat down and wrote a book that is called *Organic Growing: the Road to Survival*. Some words from the introduction are appropriate here:

> Life normally consists of a series of judgments or decisions based

on inadequate knowledge or information. This precarious situation is inescapable, and in times of real crisis can produce unbearable tensions. (One could also say that life requires learning to bear unbearable tensions.) The sounder the underlying philosophy, scale of values, principles, the more likely are the resulting guesses to be correct, or at least workable. A false philosophy, a misguided set of values, can put all satisfactory solutions out of reach.

This whole effort was triggered by a desire to help cope with the prophesies of doom which pervade the contemporary atmosphere.... In a sense they are neither true nor untrue. They are warnings.... It is extraordinary, quite unbelievable in fact, how energetically such warnings are being ignored by the powers that be.

It would be the wildest sentimental dreaming to assume that a city dweller, who has never even taken care of a house plant, can become self sufficient in feeding himself, without a considerable period of painful readjustment and much trial and error.... The following text will provide all the help I am able to offer with the practical problems of food supply, but surely it would be a most inadequate type of survival which consisted solely of keeping the belly half full and the body breathing. Surely it should not be necessary to regress all the way back to the pure brutishness of the cave man. Yet that is a danger which can be avoided only by the exertion of extreme control.

The text of the book then follows with carefully organized, right to the point, information that should be invaluable. The manuscript is in the possession of Ananda Publications and its production is planned.

For more than a decade, Haanel Cassidy was one of the key people within the community. His contribution was enormous as a teacher, as a warm and dedicated friend to everyone who truly knew him, and as a sincere and steadfast follower of the yogic path.

In the early spring of 1980 he fell ill and began to complain of severe stomach pains. Dr. Deborah Way attended him and quickly diagnosed cancer. She recommended immediate hospitalization where the best available methods of therapy could be utilized. Cassidy refused; fully aware of his condition, he made the decision to remain at Ananda where he would be among his friends and close to his beloved garden. Also, an album of his photographs was about to be published and he wanted to be free to see the project through to its conclusion.

At this point Anandi stepped in. After talking with Dr. Way, she offered to bring her sleeping bag and move into Cassidy's dome where she would be on hand to attend to him. The man who all of his life had been fiercely independent declined the offer—he would look after himself.

For a short time he continued on alone, but the community members kept dropping in several times a day, bringing him juices and food that he particularly liked. Before long he was unable to walk any more and definitely needed help. It was then that Anandi, moved in and began to look after him in a way that only a totally devoted friend could have done. She cared for him physically, fed him, and read to him every night from his favorite author: P.G. Wodehouse. As she got up repeatedly during the night, every night, to take care of her patient, Anandi often felt very strongly the presence of Yogananda. Much of the time Cassidy was in terrible agony, but he refused to take anything more than mild pain killers.

During the day, when Anandi went to work, other members of the community stayed with him so that he was attended twenty-four hours a day. He was constantly watched over by Dr. Way, but there was little she could do for him; when he asked for a reiki healer, one was provided to see him every day. Anandi slept on the floor of the living room and continuously watched over him. His son and daughter were sent for; his daughter, Sylvia, who was the particular light of his life, came from England to be at her father's bedside.

As the deadly disease ate deeper and deeper into his body, Cassidy grew mellower and mellower. He could no longer do anything physical for himself, but each morning and evening Anandi, and often others, would meditate with him. His son David, who for a time had not been on too good terms with his father, was fully reconciled.

Dr. Way and Anandi were with him one morning when he asked to have his large picture of Yogananda moved to where he could see it as he lay in bed. Then he took Anandi's hand, and held it in the grip of true and enduring friendship. In that manner, as the yogis say, he left his body. As he had asked,

Anandi bent over and chanted "Aum" softly three times in his ear. Daya Mata had done that for her guru at his request.

Anandi and Dr. Way cleaned and changed him, then with his children present, they read the Astral Ascension Ceremony. An all-night vigil was kept; the following day Kriyananda led the whole community in the Ascension Ceremony in the temple. Thus it was that Haanel Cassidy became the first, and so far the only, person to die at Ananda. It had been as he had wanted it to be. His final days were passed in unexpected comfort; Dr. Way was unable to explain how the bed sores he had developed so suddenly disappeared.

His wish was that he be cremated and his ashes scattered at Ananda. When he was sent away, his picture of his guru went with him; when his ashes came back they were taken to the grove of persimmon trees that were his especial favorites. There his closest and most beloved friends carried out his final wish.

In his life, and in his death, Haanel Cassidy personified everything that Ananda means and strives to mean. He is permanently part of the community; those who work in the garden today feel his presence. They are sure that he will be reborn in due time with a much higher and better karma. They are waiting for him to come back to Ananda in his new body. Meanwhile, he is with his guru and in that they take great comfort.

The garden at Ananda is now a great success. There are not too many men who acquire such a glowing monument.

Chapter Thirteen

Reading, Writing, and Meditation—Nitai

Since there are many children at Ananda, and a number of well qualified teachers are permanent residents, it is quite in order that the community have its own school system. And considering the fact that Ananda is first of all a spiritual yogic organization, it is to be expected that both the curriculum and the teaching methods are somewhat unconventional. What may be surprising is the fact that the Ananda schools are of a remarkably high quality and that the students they turn out are much more advanced than the great majority of their contemporaries.

Both the Ananda elementary and the high school are chartered by the State of California as legal alternatives to public education. College admissions boards treat Ananda graduates as they do students who apply from conventional schools, evaluating them on their grades, recommendations and college entrance examinations. It is significant that in the periodic examinations given to elementary school children, the Ananda pupils consistently score one or two full grades above the norm for California students as a whole. In addition, they learn to excel in many subjects which are outside the scope of regular public school education.

At the present time sixty eight students are enrolled in the Ananda schools. A fifty percent increase is anticipated with the new fall semester. Twelve full time teachers are employed and more are available as soon as they are needed. Despite the fact that free public education is available nearby, and the Ananda schools charge tuition, in 1979 two students enrolled from outside the community. In 1980 the figure rose to twelve. When the plans were laid for the fall 1981 semester, more than thirty outside students were anticipated. It has even reached the point where some families have moved into the vicinity solely so that their children can enroll in the Ananda program.

Part of this may be attributed to the ratio of fewer than twelve students per teacher which insures a high degree of personal attention for each child. Another contributing factor is the quality of the faculty. But most of all, the notable success of the Ananda schools may be credited to the basic system by which they operate, the concept of "how-to-live" education.

One evening a small group was gathered in Kriyananda's home after dinner. Most of those present were Ananda members, a few were guests from outside. The subject of the Ananda schools was under discussion. Someone went to the door in response to a ring and ushered in a young woman who had two little girls in her care, ages six and seven.

Almost at once the children were the center of attention. They were asked if they were students in the Ananda elementary school.

They were.

Would they answer some questions for the nice ladies and gentlemen?

They were willing.

When asked what they studied, they mentioned reading, writing, understanding nature, history and math. They were quiet little girls and answered in very soft voices.

That should have been enough, but one of the guests asked if they also studied yoga.

They said that they did.

What kind of yoga?

They said meditation.

Did they like it?

Yes, they did.

Did they learn any of the yoga postures in school?

Yes, they did.

Would they mind giving a little demonstration?

There was doubt at that point, largely because both of the children were very obviously not at all inclined to show off.

Oh, but please do!

In response the smaller girl placed her forearms together

on the floor at a ninety degree angle and, bending over, put her head in the apex of the triangle. Her companion did likewise. Then, straight as two little arrows, they stood motionless on their heads.

There were no further questions.

Some years before this incident Michael Deranja was a student at U.C., Berkeley. Although he graduated Phi Beta Kappa, he had not yet determined what he wanted for his career. He had a go at social work, after which he literally set out to seek his fortune. Among other things he wanted to meditate; since they meditated in India, he hitch-hiked his way there and celebrated his arrival by coming down with malaria.

After his recovery he returned to California where, in a bookstore, he found a copy of Kriyananda's *Cooperative Communities*. After reading the little book, he decided to pay Ananda a visit. He went and stayed most of the summer, but the community was then in its primitive beginnings and whatever it was he was seeking was still missing. More than anything else, he wanted to find a specific way to serve, so he returned to school and took his masters degree in education at U.C. Davis and also acquired his teaching credentials. He returned to Ananda on a Friday in 1972, started the Ananda schools on the following Monday, and has been there ever since.

The beginnings were not imposing. In the fall of 1972 six students presented themselves; they were five to seven years of age. Two teachers were ready to instruct them, but the only available classroom was a converted chicken shed which gave off constant odorous reminders of the previous occupants. Furthermore, there was no furniture of any kind and weather insulation was non-existent.

The new school did have one thing going for it: a concept of education that had never really been tested in the United States. New ideas in education appear continuously, but not all of them are successful. It has been noted that many of the children who received their primary education in the early sixties and their college educations in the seventies today in too many cases cannot write legibly or spell well enough to write a simple article.

They were in school during a period when the national $95 billion education program was developing problems that continued to grow steadily worse. Test scores dropped as student violence went on the increase. Teachers frequently reported themselves as "burned out." In urban areas drugs were peddled to school children on campus; dangerous weapons, including guns, were recovered from high school students. Integration became a key issue and forced bussing was tried out as an expedient, only to arouse strong feelings on both sides of the issue. Violence and vandalism reached the epidemic level.

Against all this Ananda had an idea that was first promulgated by Yogananda in 1917; he called it "how-to-live education" and established a school in India to bring it into being. The school prospered and did sensationally well until 1920 when its founder moved to America; after that it was never the same.

Basically Yogananda proposed an educational program that would be divided into four parts: physical, social, mental and spiritual.

The physical element was intended to promote good health and vitality, to draw on hidden reserves of energy and to bring both enthusiasm and willingness to every scholastic activity.

The social aspect was included to promote the making of genuine friendships, to emphasize standing up for true values in the face of peer pressure, to show the satisfaction that comes from helping others, and to motivate the student to look forward to contributing constructively and creatively to society.

The mental part was designed to develop reason, concentration, memory and creativity; to teach will power, the way to transform obstacles into opportunities through a positive attitude, and to help the student to rise above his emotions without at the same time stifling them.

The spiritual element was included to teach the student techniques of calming both the body and the mind. It was also designed to help him to contact the inner source of joy through meditation, and to begin to understand the relationship that exists between God and man.

Yogananda himself put it quite clearly:

> Educational authorities deem it impossible to teach spiritual principles in public school because they confuse them with the variety of religious faiths. But if they concentrate on universal principles of peace, love, service, tolerance and faith that govern the spiritual life, and devise practical methods of growing such seeds in the fertile soil of the child's mind, then the imaginary difficulty is dissolved. It is a great mistake to ignore this problem just because it is seemingly difficult.*

By the time the winter of 1972 was approaching, the impromptu schoolhouse was becoming increasingly cold. Some plain furniture had been built, but the one pathetic little heater was no match for the howling winds that blew through the schoolroom almost without slackening speed. Michael went before the village council and stated in his quiet way that something would have to be done. His mild manner did not deceive anyone; they understood. A new schoolhouse was under construction. It was nothing but a shell, but it was at least closed in. Further work would have to wait for available funds.

Michael did not wait: in the midst of a snowstorm the children picked up their little chairs and marched up a hill to their new location. When they entered, despite the early stage of construction they found a wonderful blessing to greet them—heat. And there was no more evidence of restless chickens. School went back into session.

As the school began to develop, and its facilities improved, Michael Deranja was making his own personal advancement. He received Kriya initiation and the spiritual name Nitai. He also joined the Friends of God and became a monk. He dedicated himself to the education of the young and to the spiritual development of his charges. He was a man more than ordinarily suited to the job. At the end of the one year he had put into teaching before he came to Ananda, he had invented

*Yogananda: *Blessed Life*, p. 350 in *Man's Eternal Quest*.

an awards program that proved to be a signal success. When the honor roll was read, in addition to the usual kudos, there were prizes for the most improved reader, the kindest person, and other achievements. Every child that attended went home with a prize and no one was made to feel left out.

The same kind of creative energy has consistently gone into the Ananda school program. As children will everywhere, the community's youngsters sometimes provided disciplinary problems. When two of the boys were constantly at each other, Nitai bought two pairs of boxing gloves and hung them on the wall of the schoolroom. He then announced that the next time there was trouble, he would see that it was settled once and for all, even if someone had to get hurt. The boxing gloves were never used.

In 1976, after the fire, a boys' ashram was set up. This was in essence a dormitory where the students, both from within the community and outside, could spend five nights a week with their teacher, cooking their own meals, studying and meditating together. Nitai reported, "It's been one of the most successful experiments in our schools, giving the kids a visible sense of maturity and spiritual centeredness." Later a girls' ashram was added.

At the present time there are seven classrooms in three different locations at Ananda. Because of the rapidly expanding enrollment, and the popularity of the "how-to-live" approach, a new and much larger facility is presently under construction. The former chicken coop is long gone and all the existing classrooms are well suited to their function.

There is currently a pre-school program that accepts students as young as two and sees them through until they are ready for the Ananda kindergarten. After that there is an elementary school, a junior high and an expanding high school curriculum. Nitai himself has retired from active teaching to function as principal and administrator, but he is never very far from the classroom and the children see him frequently.

At present the schools are financed 20% by the community and 80% by the modest tuition charged both Ananda children and outsiders. The current rate is $55.00 per month, and $85.00

respectively.

From the first day that a child enrolls in the Ananda schools, regardless of age, he or she begins to take part in the "how-to-live" orientation. Nitai has commented on that:

> In the public schools much emphasis is placed on *what* the child is doing. In the how to live school we watch *how* he is doing. Is he bored, working with low energy, or in a negative mood? If so this is as much reason for a teacher to intervene as if the student were having trouble with a math problem. We help the children to recognize their own reactions to things, to set high goals for themselves, to focus their energies, and to adopt positive ways of behaving.
>
> Human beings need personal contact with the teacher. If there is one teacher for math, another for history, and so forth, the teachers will never know all their students. This would be great if people were machines. You would program thirty robots, then the next programmer would add more, and so on. But people aren't robots.

If a general rule needs to be stated, then it might be that in the Ananda schools things are not imposed on the children, but are drawn out of them. In this simple fact may lie the reason why enrollment went up 70% during the summer of 1980, and why it has continued to expand as rapidly as new students can be accommodated.

Contrary to many long established educational institutions, the primary objective of the how-to-live program is not to prepare the student to become a social success. This has been compared to a gardener who cares for one branch of a tree very well but neglects the rest. At the Ananda schools a child is not treated as an intellect only, but also as a soul and a person.

It is possible, Nitai points out, for a Phi Beta Kappa to come out of school with no real control over his emotions and deficient in will power. Such an individual, despite his scholastic achievements, may not be able to control his anger, or focus his energies. Later in life, he may find himself the victim of unwanted habits.

According to the "how-to-live" philosophy, positive energy is centered, controlled and directed. It includes an understanding approach to others and finds expression in constructive achievement.

Negative energy is manifested in anger, hatred, hostility and the things that they spawn.

The how-to-live approach teaches the child, and the adult, to distinguish between the two.

The traditional academic subjects are given full attention in the Ananda schools. Nitai has stated: "Mathematics offers many opportunities for sharpening the faculties of reasoning and concentration, thus building the mental strength necessary for the expression of will power. English encourages a heightened awareness of thoughts and feelings through the challenge of expressing them in a clear and precise manner. History provides students with illustrations of the consequences of different behavior patterns. As these initial insights are refined, the student will be able to see the application of how to live principles in all areas of their studies."

It should be noted here that the brand of math taught at Ananda is called vedic. The technique comes from India and appears to be greatly superior to the traditional *nine times nine is eighty one* sort that is so painfully memorized. Children who know vedic are able to extract square roots easily in their heads and perform other calculations that would send most other students of the same age bracket fleeing to the nearest computer.

In addition to the fundamentals of reading, writing, history, math and the like, the Ananda schools teach meditation, beginning with the very youngest children. Two things are notable here: first is the fact that it works, the second is that the children enjoy it.

The initial introduction is the very simple one: the child or children are invited to sit perfectly still for just one minute. If some particular student fidgets, he is directly challenged to try to sit still for two minutes. It is made into a game with the student the key player. This technique is almost always successful.

In the first and second grades the children have a daily

satsang, a period during which they are given simple steps in awareness of nature, some group chanting (which is really singing), and a brief period of quiet time to allow them to think of suggested beautiful things. After one such session a second grader protested, "When can we have a long meditation?" Clearly he was thirsty for more.

The period that in regular schools is given over to exercises with the windows open are devoted instead to the yoga postures that are within the children's range. They vie with one another and find great joy in accomplishing such techniques as the Bow pose which is a fairly tough assignment for most athletic adults.

The channeling of positive energy at times produces some remarkable results. In the spring of 1981 the children themselves decided to have a challenge bicycle ride. They would ask local residents and merchants to sponsor them at so much per mile. One five-year old, who was the proud owner of a suitable child's bike, announced that he was in the running.

To make things easy, a one-mile course was laid out; in this way no enthusiastic rider would run out of gas, in the form of available energy, too far from home. On the appointed day the riders lined up, the five-year-old among them, and were off. The race was carefully supervised to be sure that none of the riders overdid himself or otherwise ran into trouble. Round and round the course pedalled the youngest contestant, a big smile on his face. When he was finally persuaded that he had done more than enough, he had clocked 13½ miles and was still in high spirits. The record that day, incidentally, was thirty-five miles.

In the "how-to-live" program the teacher's goal is to love every child and work for his highest welfare. This individual relationship is essential; otherwise the whole concept will fail. Suggesting to the children that it is now time to be spiritual because it is good for you will usually result in rebellion. Instead the students are drawn out until a rapport is established, then the teachings are presented. The teacher appears as a friend, not a disciplinarian. Because of this approach the Ananda children seem to agree unanimously that yoga isn't all that bad and meditation is something they like to do.

Dance, music, art and drama all have a part in the Ananda curriculum, both to encourage self expression and to cultivate self discipline. The students are encouraged to keep journals; they also participate in service projects such as cutting firewood, disposing of trash and general clean-up activities. While all this is going on the children are sharing in the life of the community where high ideals are believed in and followed.

One of the special advantages of the Ananda schools is the presence of the nationally known naturalist Joseph Cornell whose book, *Sharing Nature With Children*, has won the endorsement of the Boy and Girl Scouts of America, the National Audubon Society and many more. When it was first offered by Ananda Publications it was such an instant success it had to go back on the press almost immediately with an additional run of 50,000 copies.

This fine work richly deserves all the praise it has received. The author is an Ananda resident who is in increasing demand nationally as a lecturer. As an example of his technique, the game of "Meet a Tree" may be cited. A child, alone or from a group, is blindfolded and then led into a patch of woods. The child is then introduced to a tree and invited to find out as much about it as he or she can. The child is encouraged to feel the bark, reach around it to determine its size, and to take hold of its branches if they are within reach. When this has been done, the child is taken back to the starting point by an indirect route. The blindfold is removed and the child sets out to find "his" tree. It becomes a joyous game, one crowned with victory when the special tree is located. Months afterwards children who have played the game like to point out to others the particular tree that is their special friend.

The last major ingredient in the Ananda curriculum is character. The students are taught its true importance and how to admire real "heroes" on the sound premise that if they can be attracted by Superman they can look up to Abraham Lincoln; if they are fascinated by Batman, they can also learn the significance of Martin Luther King.

The children learn many basics, such as the fact that being

truthful is calming, while lying upsets.

From ages one to six, when children are preoccupied with the discovery of their own bodies, they are helped to understand their physical selves and their environment. From six to twelve, emphasis is laid on feeling and the value of such things as peace of mind and generosity. From twelve to eighteen prime attention is given to developing will power and the students are challenged to stretch their expanding abilities further. At this time the decision making process is taught.

The Ananda Schools also conduct training seminars for teachers and parents. These fill one week. There are three week internships for those who want to go more deeply into the "how-to-live" concept. There is also a three week apprenticeship for girls which has included a five-day backpacking trip in the High Sierras. The program also offers instruction in organic gardening, craft workshops, spiritual discussions and beginning yoga.

In his short but very definitive book, *The Art of Joyful Education,* Michael Nitai Deranja has set down the full story of the Ananda schools. In it he states:

> Over the years a definite framework has evolved for meeting the overall needs of the children.... The framework for how to live education [is] in four steps: first, that there is a dimension of consciousness underlying our lives that expands progressively from a selfish preoccupation with personal concerns to a joyous appreciation of the interdependence and oneness of all life; second, that there are a number of physical, mental, social and spiritual factors that contribute to growth along this dimension; third, that childhood offers special opportunities for development through a succession of rhythms or cycles; and fourth, that the sensitivity and awareness of the teacher is an essential ingredient in helping the child toward the realization of his highest potential.

Going to school is a process that many children begin by anticipating and before long come to look upon as an unavoidable chore that they are stuck with during the greater part of their formative years. By presenting a different form of motivation, and a curriculum to match, the Ananda schools have succeeded in giving their pupils a real thirst for knowledge and desire to learn. This achievement alone is enough to make them of unusual interest not only to educators, but also to the parents of children everywhere.

Chapter Fourteen

Industry at Ananda

Ananda is a spiritual community, but it is not one with its head in the clouds and a simple trust that the Lord will provide. As the Ananda management and residents see it, God helps those who help themselves and they therefore put a great deal of energy into their business activities. In particular, the community is dedicated to the ideal that none of its members will accept public assistance or otherwise become a burden on the other taxpayers of the county. Ananda pays its way through ingenuity and hard work, with all donations, as they may be tendered, accepted with sincere thanks.

Ever since the community was established, its financing has been precarious. There has never been a visible surplus, because there are always a number of urgent projects awaiting the moment when a few dollars may be diverted their way. In addition, thousands of dollars have had to be spent on Environment Impact Reports, Master Plans and an expensive new road, all for the purpose of meeting legal requirements. The 1976 fire was a staggering loss, and there have been other reverses, but careful management by Jyotish, Seva and the Village Council has kept things going and the community has never been in default. It has succeeded in meeting all its bills and its credit rating is solid.

Perhaps to the surprise of the public officials of Nevada County, the cash flow through Ananda already exceeds $2 million per year. In addition, the thousands of visitors who come to the community spend a great deal of money in both Nevada City and its sister city, Grass Valley. Visitors take lodgings, patronize restaurants, buy in the shops and stores, purchase tickets to various events, and have their cars tended in local garages and gas stations. While no accurate statistics are available concerning this contribution to the Nevada County economy, it is obviously substantial.

Ananda derives its income from three principal sources. The first is the businesses conducted by the community itself or, more accurately, by the Yoga Fellowship—the non-profit religious corporation that holds title to the Ananda land and the other physical assets of the community.

The second source of income is the contributions of money, goods and services by Ananda members and well-wishers. These are all gratefully received and acknowledged. A magnificent gift of $100,000 made possible the initial construction of the World Brotherhood Retreat. Many other gifts, some of very modest amounts, have all helped substantially in the development and growth of the community.

The third source of income is the approximately thirty different businesses privately owned and operated by resident members. These bring cash and credit into the community, and almost all of the owners tithe their profits for the benefit of the Fellowship.

Ananda never overlooks an opportunity to turn an honest dollar. When Kriyananda went to Australia in 1980 he purchased at wholesale a small quantity of opals of very high quality and turned them over to the community for sale. Although they were expensive, a number of residents and visitors recognized them as exceptional buys at the prices asked. The resulting funds went into the Fellowship treasury.

It is significant that whenever two possible projects come up, one that may prove profitable and one that will benefit the spiritual life of the community, the latter is always chosen. The first priority at Ananda is always spiritual growth; the second is trying to help an individual. The resident M.D.s, for example, are never asked to go out and earn funds for the community; their spiritual welfare is considered much more important.

Ananda has long had it in mind to set up a reserve or an endowment fund, but the clear opportunity to do so has never presented itself. Since the community needs are so many, particularly with its present rate of growth, an endowment fund will probably be established when some donations are received for that specific purpose, and no other.

Of the cash producing activities conducted by the community itself, one of the most successful is the Meditation Retreat. It is now operated as a year-round program with a staff of twelve. It would be even more popular were it not for the agreement with the Bald Mountain Association which, for all practical purposes, prohibits any expansion or improvement of the existing facilities. This restriction was a major factor in the decision to build the new, and very much better, World Brotherhood Center and Retreat at The Farm. It is not only far more spacious, but also superior in several other ways.

Of the many courses and programs offered by the Retreat, the Yoga Teachers' Training Course is the most popular, but there are also substantial enrollments in vegetarian cooking, hatha yoga (the postures), meditation and a number of other subjects. Many of the students return year after year and bring their friends with them. One of the advantages of enrolling at the Retreat is the opportunity to experience Ananda, to attend some of the community's functions, and to meet various of the permanent residents.

Quite often persons who had come to the Retreat searching for something find it and remain to become members of the community.

Another major activity is Ananda Publications and Recordings, or Pubble, as it is locally known. Its impressive building fits beautifully into the landscape, looking serene on the outside, but a literal beehive of activity within. There are offices and work spaces in every nook and cranny of the building which has a truncated second story in which Shivani, now the general manager of Pubble, holds forth.

Twenty or twenty-five people work at Pubble in a wide variety of jobs. There are graphic designers, editors, pressmen, layout and paste-up personnel, artists, clerical workers and secretaries. There is also a mailing department and the staff of Ananda Recordings that publishes both records and tapes.

Much of the material turned out by Pubble is by

Kriyananda; all of his books and essays are normally available, although some occasionally go out of print. But there is also a great deal of additional material. The newsletters and bulletins of the Friends of Ananda are produced here, as are the brochures for the Meditation Retreat and the Apprentice Program.

One of the outstanding products of Pubble, and one that was produced entirely in house, is the much acclaimed *Sharing Nature with Children,* by Joseph Bharat Cornell. Another excellent little work is *The Art of Joyful Education,* by Michael Nitai Deranja, the principal of the Ananda schools. This very engaging discussion of education is much enhanced by the sensitive drawings of Elizabeth Ann Kelley.

Two of the cornerstone offerings by Pubble are Kiryananda's *The Path: Autobiography of a Western Yogi* and the popular correspondence course, *Fourteen Steps to Perfect Joy.* Ananda Publications also prepares booklets and brochures about the community and, in response to many requests, its requirements for membership. It is never short of material to produce; the limiting factors are frequently press time and cash flow, a perennial problem with most expanding businesses. When Shivani received a sizable legacy from a member of her family, she promptly put it into the business so that some waiting projects could be expedited.

Ananda Publications puts out an attractive catalog that can be had for the asking.

All this may conjure up the picture of a hard-nosed, money-making business, but that is an illusion. Almost all the decisions taken by Shivani and the other management personnel are based on spiritual rather than commercial considerations; providing a needed service ranks above turning a fast profit. Also, there are not too many publishing and printing organizations that shut down at the height of their activity to allow time for both lunch and midday meditation. The plant is full of pin-ups, as would be expected, but the ladies who adorn *Penthouse* and *Playboy* are not represented. There is not a room or office that does not display a picture of Yogananda and usually one or more of the other great yoga teachers. There are also portraits of a scattering of Catholic saints (St. Theresa is the favorite), James Lynn, the late President of the Self Realization Fellowship, and Sri Daya Mata, who succeeded him. Portraits of Christ are also much in evidence.

Far more modest in size, but an integral part of the community, is the Ananda Dairy. The dairy maintains cows, goats and chickens (for eggs) and turns out a variety of products including milk, yogurt, cottage cheese and other items, most of which are sold in Master's Market. The dairy staff is well aware of modern methods of increasing milk production through the use of feed urea and certain drugs, but refuses to use them for fear that in some way they might get into the milk or other products.

Master's Market is a grocery and general store that is showing an impressive rate of growth. In 1978 it grossed $100,000; in 1979 it was up to $156,000; in 1980 it was well over $200,000 per annum. Much of the produce sold at the market comes from the Ananda gardens and, despite the poor soil, is of excellent quality. The market is located in what was originally the farmhouse and is part of what is known as Downtown Ananda. It is primarily operated for the benefit of the community, but is open to the public. Quite a few of Ananda's neighbors drop by to purchase items. Most of the canned and packaged foods are of the "health" variety; the root beer to be found in the refrigerated cabinet is made with honey.

There is a kitchen in back of Master's Market that serves a well patronized noon meal—vegetarian, of course. It is a major improvement over the original outdoor kitchen which was principally noted for an open fire and bees.

The community operates two businesses in Nevada City proper, the Mountain Song Handcraft store, which does moderately well, and the Earth Song health food store and restaurant which has proved to be a major success. When it started in 1978 its entire assets were $14,000 including stock and equipment. By 1980 it was averaging close to $1,000 a day in sales and increasing steadily. Ananda also serves Nevada City with the Yoga Fellowship Church which was acquired from another congregation in 1981.

In 1980 Ananda bought the East-West Bookstore in Menlo Park, California, and took over its operation. Not to be outdone, the Ananda House in San Francisco started a restaurant.

All of these projects not only generate cash flow for the community, but they also provide employment opportunities for its members. At the present time approximately 80% of the adult Ananda residents work for the community in some capacity. Quite frequently there are more job opportunities than there are qualified people to fill them.

Another source of revenue for the community's coffers is membership fees and the monthly rental paid by the resident members. In the latter cases, these are so nominal that they are not a substantial factor. Since membership is a one-time fee, this too is a strictly limited source of income.

In addition to the community's own ventures, there are many privately owned and operated businesses based at Ananda. An important one is the Ananda Construction Company headed by Arthur Lucki who, when he is overburdened with blueprints and cost estimates, can take refuge in the fact that he is Shivani's husband. The Ananda builders have erected many homes in the greater Nevada City area and have earned a solid reputation for sound construction and a blessed absence of corner cutting. Its most important undertaking to date is the World Brotherhood Retreat which, when it is finally completed, will be a $2 million project.

One of the advantages of doing business with the Ananda Construction Company is the firm's in-house capability for producing designs, cabinetry, stained glass windows, blacksmith items and many other components needed for a quality custom house.

In 1979 the many cottage industries at Ananda combined into a federation called the Joyful Crafts and Arts Guild. Various of the individual proprietors work in weaving, jewelry manufacturing, leatherware, incense and oils, yoga clothing (don't try to do the Plow pose in your best Sunday suit), photo typesetting design, and macrame. Products made by Ananda craftsmen are sold in such San Francisco stores as Macy's, The

City of Paris and The Emporium.

Ananda is also the permanent home of a fine artist whose paintings command impressive prices in the Los Angeles galleries and elsewhere. Ever since his high school days in Portland, Oregon, Eric Estep had been studying yoga and preparing himself for a lifestyle that would be built around a forest setting free from urban distractions where he could devote a major part of his time to contemplation. To prepare himself for this, he spent many months camping in the mountains and learning survival skills.

While he was attending the California College of Arts and Crafts he began visiting the services offered by the Self Realization Fellowship. However, in his own words, "I found many of the SRF functions a bit too stuffy and dogmatic for my taste." He was about to abandon his study of the teachings of the Yogananda entirely when, again to quote him, "I heard Swamiji's name whispered at the SRF center. I was naturally curious to meet him."

He did meet Kriyananda and learned from him that a community was about to be formed near Nevada City, a small hermitage where people would be able to live simply and spend as much time as they liked in meditation. Estep did not need to hear any more: in the summer of 1969, its first year, he moved to Ananda which was then in a very primitive state. Few were capable of enjoying the living conditions that prevailed there at the time, but it suited him perfectly. He built himself a minimal home and an even smaller studio and took up the lifestyle of which he had always dreamed. He received Kriya initiation and the spiritual name of Sundaram.

Quiet, soft spoken, and very much his own man, Sundaram is more than satisfied with his establishment at the Meditation Retreat. It is buried deep among the trees, well out of sight of casual visitors. Those invited guests who call invariably find him a charming and delightful host. In his studio, if he elects to show them, he usually has canvases, not yet delivered, that reveal the work of a remarkably creative mind. He is especially gifted in painting the great peaks of the Himalaya, although he has yet to see them in actuality. He also upon occasion produces fanciful landscapes that give tantalizing glimpses of a totally different world. These, especially, are in considerable demand.

Sundaram has done a series of portraits of the great masters of yoga which an informed critic would probably find superior to those available elsewhere. Prints of some of these works can be bought from Ananda. Other striking paintings by him of Yogananda, Swami Sri Yuteswar, and other venerated gurus are to be found in the Ananda temple and in the World Brotherhood Retreat.

Not every business that has been launched at Ananda has prospered, but the great majority have succeeded, one reason being that overhead costs are normally extraordinarily low. As the community continues to expand, it is inevitable that among the newcomers will be professionals, craftsmen and others well qualified to go into a business of their own. This type of enterprise is encouraged and assisted by the Promotions Department which currently has a staff of five capable people.

Ananda is presently still producing more Environment Impact Reports and other documentation that involves heavy expense. Mercifully, the end of all this is in sight. When that happy day dawns, Ananda may well find itself in a much more comfortable financial position. The funds now being expended on legal matters will be available instead to meet many other pending requirements. At the same time the solid success of such enterprises as Earth Song can be expected to produce greater revenues and the establishment of sinking funds for such projects as the much-needed new monastery.

Ordinarily financial discussions are likely to be somewhere between dry as dust and utterly boring. It is not so at Ananda, for in everything that the community undertakes there seems to be a built-in element of adventure, with the kind of risks that the very word adventure implies. And, perhaps miraculously, no matter what has happened, or what disasters have struck, Ananda has always managed, somehow, to come up with the cold hard cash when necessity has dictated. There are a great many managers of other enterprises who would like to have the same magic touch. Or, perhaps, the same guru.

Chapter Fifteen

For the Chosen—Kriya Yoga

The beginnings of Kriya Yoga are lost in antiquity. It is reputed that Lord Krishna taught the secret to his disciple, Arjuna, but enjoined him to pass it on only to those who were worthy to receive it. Its history during the following centuries is not known: like many other lost arts or pieces of ancient wisdom, it apparently died out completely and vanished from the face of the earth.

Fortunately, the basic forms of yoga did not; they were actively practiced and taught as the centuries of India's history rolled by. In the seventh century yoga passed into China and soon after that it reached Japan. Its virtues were quickly recognized and it was continued with surprisingly little modification up to the present time.

The Kriya technique reappeared under rather remarkable circumstances. The great *Yogavatar* (Incarnation of Yoga) Lahiri Mahasaya (1828-1895) was a pupil and disciple of the deathless Babaji. Babaji, whose own origins are unrecorded, was in possession of the ancient secret and deemed it time that it should be given back to the world. He therefore revealed it to Mahasaya with specific instructions to pass it on to those who were spiritually prepared to receive it.

This the great teacher certainly did. It is reputed that during his lifetime he gave Kriya initiation to more than 100,000 persons. As was consistent with his character, he did not discriminate against anyone and taught the technique equally not only to Hindus, but also to Muslims and Christians. This householder saint was not one to withhold a blessing from anyone who he could perceive would benefit from it. Because of his generosity in sharing what he knew to be a

181

great gift to mankind, the ancient science of Kriya took a firm fresh root in the land of its origin.

Swami Sri Yukteswar was a disciple of Mahasaya and received instruction in Kriya from him. He, in turn, initiated his pupil Yogananda with the special added instruction that he was to take the secret to the new world and there make it available to those qualified to receive it. Reputedly, Yogananda was prepared for this mission on the specific instructions of Babaji who had selected him for this most important assignment.

According to the Self Realization Fellowship, Paramhansa Yogananda personally gave Kriya initiation to 100,000 Americans. This means that the Indian master had to initiate an average of more than 260 people a month, during each month of his presence in this country. It is a recorded fact that he gave many initiations, but it is remarkable that he was able to give his personal attention to such a quantity of converts, particularly in view of the fact that he spent the last years of his life away from the public most of the time, devoting himself to writing and teaching his immediate disciples.

It should also be noted here that Kriya cannot be obtained simply by requesting it; a period of preparation is required and some of the rules currently followed were, according to SRF, set down by Yogananda himself.

During his lifetime, Yogananda authorized a few carefully selected disciples who were very advanced in yoga to conduct the sacred initiation ceremony. One of these was Kriyananda. Subsequent to the Master's passing, a few others have been admitted to the ranks of those permitted to give initiation into the Kriya. At the present time Kriya initiation may be received at the Self Realization Fellowship and at Ananda. As far as can be determined, the initiation ceremony is given nowhere else in this country, although there are a few individuals who know the technique and who have undertaken to teach it.

It has been said by Kriyananda that Kriya Yoga is the cement that holds Ananda together. Most of the resident members have received initiation, practice the technique regularly, and have seen it produce a major change in their lives. It would not be an exaggeration to say that the encompassing feeling of joy that so pervades Ananda is a direct result of the practice of the Kriya.

Kriya itself is a specific technique of meditation that controls the breath and produces a flow of balanced energy up and down the spine. This information is given in the chapter on Kriya Yoga in *Autobiography of a Yogi*. In the same work, Yogananda states, "Kriya Yoga is a simple, psychophysiological method by which human blood is decarbonated and recharged with oxygen."

Yogananda also quotes his guru, Swami Sri Yukteswar, as stating, "Kriya Yoga is an instrument through which human evolution can be quickened. The ancient yogis discovered that the secret of cosmic consciousness is intimately linked with breath mastery. This is India's unique and deathless contribution to the world's treasury of knowledge. The life force, which is ordinarily absorbed in maintaining heart action, must be freed for higher activities by a method of calming and stilling the ceaseless demands of the breath."

The above quotation is slightly misleading: the Kriya technique as taught at Ananda, and at the Self Realization Fellowship, does not require stopping the breath, or the holding of breath for any extended period of time.

As a technique, the Kriya is considered immensely powerful. In the chapter cited, Yogananda makes this startling statement: "In three years a Kriya yogi (who practices 8½ hours per day) can accomplish by intelligent self effort the same result that nature brings to pass in a million years." The word of such an authority is not to be questioned. Later he supplies an interesting comparison as well as some instruction:

Introspection, or 'sitting in silence,' is an unscientific way of trying to force apart the mind and senses, tied together by the life force. The contemplative mind, attempting its return to Divinity, is constantly dragged back toward the senses by the life currents. Kriya, controlling the mind *directly* through the life force, is the easiest, most effective, and most scientific avenue of approach to the Infinite. In contrast to the slow, uncertain 'bullock cart' theological path to God, Kriya Yoga may justly be called the 'airplane' route.

The entire chapter on Kriya in the *Autobiography* will be found of interest. The Self Realization Fellowship also has available a tape by Brother Anandamoy called *Kriya Yoga, Gateway to the Infinite* which gives additional information. A chapter on Kriya is in *The Path* and there is a brief one in Kamala's book *Priceless Precepts*. In none of these publications cited is the actual technique described.

There is also a book called *New Light on Kriya Yoga* by Swami Premananda which is actually a translation by the author of the three upanishads which, in his words, "deal directly with the way, the ritual, and the revelation of Kriya Yoga to Sri Sri Shyamacharan Lahiri (Mahasaya)." Unfortunately the title of the book is misleading; it contains hardly anything at all about the Kriya or the method by which it is performed.

The actual technique of Kriya is secret. However, as has been the case with other restricted information, the method has been published, in at least three different places. There is a volume produced in English in India which supplies many different techniques of meditation. The Kriya is one of them, but it is not identified by name. In at least one book available in the United States the *modus operandi* is both identified and given, although not in complete detail. And, several years ago, an underground newspaper gave a full account of the Kriya method.

Apart from these departures, and possibly some others, the secret of the Kriya has been kept. Why this has been considered necessary is not entirely clear, but it would be reasonable to assume that Kriya should not be practiced until the subject is fully prepared to understand it and to utilize it properly. This requires a grounding in meditation, usually employing the *Hong Sau* and *Aum* techniques, both of which are open and fully available. In addition, the subject should be spiritually prepared to receive so powerful a tool and to benefit fully from the results it can bring.

In his book *Ananda Cooperative Village: A Study on the Beliefs, Values and Attitudes of a New Age Religious Community* (Uppsala, Sweden, 1978), Ted A. Nordquist states: "One can say that *self realization* is the ultimate goal and that the term implies a belief in the concept of *God* and *creation,* while *devotion to God* and the technique of *Kriya Yoga* provide the means of attaining this goal.

"Kriya Yoga is the method by which the devotee can realize union with God."

Normally the Kriya technique is only given through initiation. This is a very moving ceremony which most participants approach with a full realization of its significance. In the words of one young woman at Ananda: "I was twenty four and had been at Ananda for two years when, in the spring, I was to take Kriya. I felt that this would probably be the most significant moment of my life. To prepare myself I went into a ten day withdrawal, fasting and in silence. I was single and living in a trailer. When I went up for the blessing my heart was pounding; I didn't think I would make it up there. It was a magical blessing of my life. Meditation is now much easier, as if God were giving me encouragement."

Govinda stated: "I was initiated in August 1975. At that time I made an eternal bond to God and the masters. It grew and is still growing. When I do Kriya now, I feel such a rush of energy and joy going up my spine, it can't be described in words."

John Novak: "It was the turning point of my life. It has produced a gradual, but very total change. The Kriya is my link to God through Master. It has become the central core of my existence."

Vijay said simply: "Kriya is holy. It is God's presence right there."

Initiation into Kriya yoga can be obtained at Ananda, or through the Self Realization Fellowship. Anyone may subscribe to the mail order lessons that the Fellowship offers. They are sent out at weekly intervals; they run an average of seven pages each and are made available at moderate cost. The first series consists of twenty-eight lessons plus an additional four summaries, a total of thirty-two weeks. At this point the student receives a brief questionnaire consisting of six easy questions which is to be filled out and sent in to the Fellowship headquarters, commonly known as the Mother Center. Whether the student complies or not, he is welcome to renew his subscription for the next series of lessons.

With lesson number S-2-52 he receives a second examination which contains five more simple questions that anyone who has even skimmed the lessons should be able to answer. The student also receives with this lesson an invitation to apply for Kriya Yoga and a Kriya pledge to be signed and sent in. Upon receipt of both questionnaires and the signed pledge, the student is then normally sent a special series of lessons that contains the full details of the Kriya technique. He is also invited to attend an initiation ceremony at the Mother Center or other SRF facility. This is all that is required.

When asked, an SRF spokesman stated that a student is often accepted for Kriya initiation in less time than it takes to reach this point in the lessons if the minister in charge of his church, or another qualified person, decides that he is ready to attend the sacred ceremony and to be given the technique. Receiving Kriya from the Self Realization Fellowship is, therefore, a fairly simple matter. It is even possible for an insincere person to abuse the trust of the Fellowship and attend a Kriya ceremony through simple misrepresentation. Hopefully, such instances are rare.

At Ananda, Kriya initiation is normally given only twice each year, once in the spring and at the conclusion of the annual Spiritual Renewal Week in the early fall. Candidates for initiation must meet the following qualifications: be studying the SRF lessons (no specific number is required), be studying or have completed the *Fourteen Steps to Perfect Joy*, have read *Autobiography of a Yogi*, and have been actively practicing meditation, preferably using both the *Hong Sau* and *Aum* techniques. A formal letter of application must also be submitted. There is some flexibility in these requirements to fit individual cases. Normally, prior to initiation each candidate has a personal meeting with Kriyananda at which time his qualifications for initiation are reviewed and he is told whether or not he has been accepted.

If the candidate is successful, and with very few exceptions they are, he is then asked to observe certain procedures. On the day of his initiation insofar as practical he or she is to remain in seclusion. The candidate is also asked to observe silence, speaking only if necessary, and to fast throughout the day. Those who for physical reasons cannot go without food for this period of time are allowed fruit or fruit juices. It is also the custom at Ananda for those who are to be initiated, and those already initiated who will be attending the ceremony, to dress entirely in white except for the Friends of God who wear renunciate yellow. All candidates are expected to remain as quiet as possible and to spend as much time as they are able in meditation. A few choose to walk alone in silence in the woods.

The candidates gather in strict silence on the large deck of the common dome, directly adjacent to the temple. There they sit in meditation, and it would be an unfeeling person indeed who would not sense the rich aura that surrounds them. They begin to arrive at a little after five; by five thirty they are all there.

Throughout the day Kriyananda will have been maintaining a strict seclusion, preparing himself for the very solemn occasion over which he will preside. He has spoken of this, saying, "What I feel is that God is using me as an instrument. I can feel the blessings flow through me. It has been a very important factor in the lives of the initiates and of the community.

"The power of blessing is something independent of me. When the time comes for the Kriya to start, then it's there. Often during the afternoon I feel completely alone, but when six o'clock comes, I feel that the masters are there with me."

Just at six a gong sounds four times; those who have been waiting rise and file silently into the temple for one of the great experiences of their lives. Normally, Keshava, secretary to Kriyananda, stands at the door and checks each person who enters to be sure that he or she is on the list of the accepted candidates. When the last person has passed inside, the doors are closed. No one is admitted after that, regardless of circumstances.

The Kriya initiation ceremony takes approximately three hours. Basically it consists of three parts. After the brief opening hymns, or chants, there is a fire ceremony which influences the karma of all those who have been admitted. Karma is a law, normally inviolate, through which each person builds for himself an accounting of both the good and the bad that he does during his lifetime. A very few individuals, Christ being the outstanding One, lead lives of such selfless service to others they acquire enough good karma in one lifetime to bring them the great goal toward which all of mankind is seen to be striving—union with God.

For the rest, the wheel of karma turns and they are reborn, according to yogic belief, to build more good karma and to expiate the bad through sacrifice and good deeds. This cycle may continue through hundreds of lifetimes until freedom is finally earned and the soul is no longer subject to the relentless repetition of suffering and rebirth.

During the fire ceremony that is part of the Kriya initiation the karma of those who are present undergoes a change: the fire consumes much if not all of the bad karma they have accumulated. This is made possible through the benevolence and God-given power of the masters, much as sins are forgiven during regular Christian worship.

After this, each initiate is required to take certain very serious lifetime vows. The first is a permanent commitment of allegiance to the line of six gurus that ended with Yogananda. The second vow is never to reveal the secret of the Kriya to anyone, unless authorized to do so. The third and final one is a promise before God to practice the Kriya technique, health and circumstances permitting, each morning and evening for the rest of his or her natural life.

Following this, each person attending the ceremony presents himself individually before Kriyananda to receive the Kriya baptism and the blessing granted by the masters, through him. Some who have experienced this have said that the energy received almost knocked them off their feet. It is at this moment that each initiate is formally accepted as a permanent disciple of Paramhansa Yogananda.

When the blessings have been given, and each individual has been baptized, then the secret of the Kriya is revealed and the technique explained. A beverage is served that has a very special significance and the ceremony concludes with the singing of the Rose Chant, which is done only at Kriya. As he is baptized, each initiate is given a handful of rose petals to be kept permanently. In times of great stress or trouble, the petals will remind him that he has been blessed and that the gurus are helping him, no matter how deep his distress.

The initiate has then been accepted into God's presence and the "portals of the infinite" have been opened to him.

Because the acceptance of Kriya initiation involves lifetime obligations, each person should consider this carefully before making application. Undoubtedly some kriyabans have dropped away from the Path, just as many others have abandoned religious commitments they made either in youth or in adulthood, but no one should take Kriya initiation unless he or she fully intends to live up to the obligations that are involved.

Kriya should not be regarded as being similar to Confirmation or Bar Mitzvah, despite the fact that all three involve a religious acceptance. It is closer, perhaps, to the ceremonies when men and women enter holy orders, in that it is a much more solemn and serious occasion. No spectators are permitted; those present are either undergoing initiation or are already accepted and practicing kriyabans.

It is most advisable that husband and wife take Kriya together, unless one partner has no interest in following the Path. Otherwise serious consequences can result. There was such an incident at Ananda that was not Kriyananda's fault, but one which was very nearly responsible for a spiritual catastrophe.

A husband and wife, deeply devoted to each other, had been coming to Ananda for some two and a half years. For many months both had been intensively preparing for Kriya initiation and both had more than fulfilled the requirements. The wife had chosen to put behind her a lifetime of dedicated church-going to come onto the Path. The husband, a man much inclined to keep his deep spiritual convictions within himself, had been meditating for many years. In studying the life and works of Yogananda he found the guru he had been seeking.

When the wife wrote her letter of application for Kriya initiation, the husband wrote his on the same day and mailed them together. Only one was delivered; the husband's letter miscarried and was later returned to the sender.

Both husband and wife knew Kriyananda well and had entertained him in their home. Two days before the initiation, at the appointed time they presented themselves together to receive their final answer. Both were confident of a favorable response. Kiryananda granted a short private interview to the wife and told her she had been accepted. When the husband then asked for his interview, Kriyananda did not understand. He had been erroneously informed that the husband was a devotee of another path and since he had not received a letter of application, he had no reason to believe that the husband's application was seriously intended. He therefore did not grant the interview; instead he said to the husband. "Go and prepare yourself." In making his decision, Kriyananda certainly never intended the disaster that followed.

Unfortunately, his answer, which was meant to be a refusal, was ambiguous and the husband, understanding that he had been accepted, did not press his case further. Throughout the night before the ceremony, while his wife slept, he sat in meditation, preparing himself for what was to be the joint climax of their spiritual lives.

On Kriya day both fasted, remained silent, and shared each other's company until it was time to go to the temple. On the decking of the common dome they sat side by side in deep meditation until the gong sounded. Then, together, they joined the silent procession to the door of the temple. As the wife passed inside she was almost shaking with her awareness of the great event in her life that was about to take place. When her husband stepped up to follow her, he was turned away. Kriyananda had refused him and he was not on the list to be admitted.

Under the belief that her husband had chosen not to come with her, the wife found a place in the last row, seated herself for her Kriya toward which she had worked so long and so faithfully, and broke into tears. Her initiation, which was to have been such a wondrous event, was robbed of its magic; later she wrote to Kriyananda that the experience had been so traumatic for her it had been "like a little death."

Meanwhile her husband, in a state of disbelief and shock, seated himself on the decking near the temple, certain that the apparent mistake would quickly be detected and he would be permitted to rejoin his wife. He had shared with her such a total sense of dedication, his mind refused to accept what had happened. Even when the singing began within the temple, and he could hear it faintly outside, he still could not believe that he and his wife were not to take their Kriya initiation together.

For three long, excruciating hours he remained there while the day gradually faded and slowly gave way to night. As the darkness closed in around him, his last desperate hopes of being belatedly allowed to be with his wife in the temple could no longer survive. He did his best to send his love in to her. He managed to keep himself under control, fighting for the peace of meditation, until at last the doors were opened and the haunting Rose Chant echoed in the night.

When he heard the music, and understood its meaning, all of his spiritual aspirations, so long nurtured, deserted him. Utterly heartbroken, he lost control of his nerves and began to shake in uncontrollable spasms. He was in that condition when his wife found him.

Some who had witnessed this notified Kiryananda as soon as he came out of the temple, exhausted after the long ceremony. Despite his fatigue, he asked to see both the husband and wife as soon as possible. The little office dome was quickly cleared for his use. The discovery of what had happened must have been almost as much of a shock to him as it had been to the distraught couple that came before him. To help mitigate the disaster he spoke some words of comfort, then he placed his thumb against the husband's forehead and bestowed on him a blessing similar to the Kriya baptism.

Disappointments, tragedies, and even traumas come to many people, but mercifully almost all of them are abated by time. Kriya initiation, however, is another matter because it changes the life of the participant from the first day forward. In this instance the husband and wife, who were profoundly close to each other, were forcefully separated by a chasm that unavoidably widened each day. Every morning and night, true to her vow, the wife had to seclude herself to practice the Kriya technique she could not share with her husband. He, in turn, found himself blocked out of the meditation techniques he had been practicing for many years and spiritually impotent. Both husband and wife tried desperately to put the matter behind them, but at least twice a day it had to come to the fore. As the weeks passed the husband noted some significant changes in his wife as a result of her Kriya practice, but it was something he could not share.

When he became fully aware of the circumstances, Kriyananda did everything he possibly could to rectify the unbearable situation. Against all precedent he scheduled a special Kriya initiation at a time when it is normally never given. On that occasion the husband and wife sat together, hand in hand, in seats that had been reserved for them in the foremost row. In support of them more than a hundred of their Ananda friends fasted all day, kept silence, and came to the ceremony. As far as is known, the husband was the only initiate. According to the wife, who reluctantly consented to discuss the matter, it was an inspirited initiation and for the first time she experienced the true meaning of the Kriya.

Some months later, knowing that the emotional trauma suffered by both the husband and wife was deep-set and still causing them serious spiritual problems, Kriyananda invited them to his home as houseguests so that they could meditate with him. Such an invitation was unprecedented at Ananda. At that time, in Kriyananda's dome and with the benefit of his presence both husband and wife made a supreme effort. An event then occurred of a near miraculous nature, but those concerned have asked that it not be made public. Suffice it to say that the fabric of the two deeply distressed lives was woven back together once again and the anguishing problem was mitigated.

It is most unlikely that this will ever happen again at Ananda. Those who think of the Kriya as only a meditation method would be well advised to leave it strictly alone. But for those, like the residents of Ananda, who feel the true importance of God in their lives, it is a powerful and sacred technique by means of which doors may be opened, the Infinite beheld, and the Path to a more wonderful and joyous life unrolled before the feet of the traveler.

Chapter Sixteen

Kriyananda

The fact that Ananda exists at all, and the record of its remarkable success as a yogic community, is due almost entirely to the work and dedication of one man—Kriyananda. It is impossible to belittle the many wholehearted devotees who have put so much of their lives and energy into the creation and continuation of Ananda; their contribution has been immense. But it is safe to say that if it had not been for Kriyananda all this would not have been done in the manner that it was and much of the property on which the community now makes its home would still be a pig and pheasant farm.

The most important single fact to be noted about Kriyananda is a negative one, but vital to understanding him as a man: he is not a charlatan. He is, perhaps, the direct opposite of the late Rev. Jim Jones in both personality and outlook. What happened at Jonestown is so remote from Ananda as to be inconceivable. Kriyananda is an utterly sincere man of deep and total commitment to God and guru. This, however, does not prevent him from being human and that he most certainly is.

A lady who knows him well, and who is a kriyaban, described him in these words:

> He has a great deal of personal magnetism. He is a very approachable person and when you speak with him, you note the steady gaze of his eyes. There is a depth to his voice and it has a comforting tone that is very reassuring. He gives you an impression of strength and stability and the feeling that he is listening to you on a one-to-one basis. You feel that whoever you are, he likes you.

As this book is written, Kriyananda is in his fifties. He

appears robust, although he is not known to take much exercise. There is a stationary bicycle in his living quarters, but if he uses it at all it is not possible to say. Almost all the time he dresses in conventional clothing; normally a shirt tucked in at the belt line, a pair of trousers, and such footgear as may be convenient for him at the moment.

He has a quick and ready smile that is much in evidence. Those who have known him over a period of years speak frequently of his energy and good disposition. He has most certainly been upset at times, usually with good reason, but he is apparently all but immune to anger. He can, if in his opinion the occasion requires, write a fairly sharp letter, but it would be difficult to imagine him enraged, even to the point of raising his voice.

The fact that he is an American rather than an Indian he recognizes as something of a two-edged sword. He is fully aware that in the public mind a swami must necessarily come from India, but this is obviously a fallacy despite the fact that he is close to unique in being a prominent American swami before the public. The word maestro was for some time largely reserved for Italian musicians; today such distinguished conductors as Leonard Bernstein, Herbert von Karajan and Seiji Ozawa are undisputed maestri despite the fact that none of these distinguished gentlemen happens to be Italian.

Kriyananda commented on this point for the purpose of this book. "There are different audiences," he said. "There are audiences who want incense, beads, and long flowing robes. To those people my being an American has been a slight disadvantage, although if I do appear in long flowing robes they appear to be satisfied. The audience I'm trying to reach is made up of Americans who aren't trying to do something exotic, they're only trying to spiritualize their own lives in their own context. To these people I can speak much more easily than could an Indian swami. I have been told many times, 'You present the teachings in a way to make them acceptable to us'."

In communication skills there is no question that Kriyananda is remarkable. He has lectured in public with major success in five languages. In addition to his language capabilities, he is highly articulate and has an almost priceless gift for being able to think on his feet. He is so good at it, in fact, that he never prepares himself by writing an outline beforehand or even developing a set of notes. When the time comes he addresses himself to his subject and almost invariably produces a memorable lecture. Many of the tapes that Ananda offers of talks by him are taken directly from his public appearances. In most instances this has worked out well; there are a few exceptions which the recording section is planning to correct. In almost all cases the problem lies not in Kriyananda's eloquence, but in the fact that under the inspiration of the moment, and the reactions of his audience, he chose to depart from his announced subject. In mitigation it should be pointed out that there is hardly a professional speaker, or similarly qualified individual, who does not at one time or another do the same thing.

Kriyananda is a man who has lived to see his dream come true. This is a rare privilege and he knows it. There is also no doubt whatever that it was his own hard work, determination and the inspiration that he gave to others that made it possible. During the early days of Ananda he almost singlehandedly undertook the job of meeting the mortgage payments of $2000 per month. While others helped, he earned the bulk of the money by maintaining an almost killing schedule of lectures and classes, and the writing of books, in an all-out effort to keep the community alive.

It is relatively easy to divide his life into specific segments. The first is, of course, his upbringing in Europe and the United States, his formal education, and his indoctrination into a variety of languages. By the time that he was twenty-two and had discovered *Autobiography of a Yogi*, he had already developed a considerable individuality, but he was prepared to earn his living either as a playwright or as a common seaman. He had not by then fully resolved his aspirations, but he had acquired an asset that was not only to shape his future life, but also to make possible many of his achievements—the ability to make a decision.

The second stage of his life began when he decided that

Paramhansa Yogananda was his guru and that he would have to hasten to his side without delay. He not only did so; he never for a moment looked back. He entered the Self Realization Fellowship as has been recounted and advanced rapidly within that organization. He learned very quickly, while his dedication deepened and his devotion to his guru grew into what any yogi would recognize as a permanent relationship. At the same time his unique talents, and distinctive personality, developed with his growing maturity.

In such a vital individual, with such wide-ranging interests, the seeds of monkhood are not likely to sprout, but from the moment he presented himself to Yogananda, he was fully prepared to forego the pleasures and satisfaction of wife and family in the fuller pursuit of his spiritual goals. Yogananda must have seen this, as evidenced by the fact that he accepted the new recruit so swiftly.

After his guru's death, Kriyananda was as emotionally distressed as the rest of the Fellowship, but there was never any question about carrying on the Indian mystic's work. There is no need to detail here the facts of Kriyananda's life during this period; they are fully covered in *The Path*. It is appropriate to note that when he returned from India to become Vice President of the Fellowship, he was the only man on the board. The management of the Fellowship was almost entirely feminine and it remains so to this day.

This period in Kriyananda's life ended with his abrupt termination with the Fellowship. A reasonable examination of the available facts concerning the schism leads to the belief that Kriyananda was treated in an underservedly harsh manner. Tara, who was undoubtedly the architect of his dismissal, died a few years later of a massive stroke. She lingered for some time in a deplorable condition before she finally passed on and joined her guru.

In speaking of her, Kriyananda said, "The truth is, I loved Tara, but had always known that we would clash one day. We stood for completely different, and incompatible, views of the work: I for reaching out to people, she for protecting the work from their diluting influence."

In his autobiography, *The Path,* Kriyananda speaks several times of his friend and fellow disciple Henry Schaufelberger, now Brother Anandamoy. On page 397 he wrote, "Henry's presence was a great blessing for me. During the weeks we spent together out there we became fast friends; our mutual attunement developed until it often happened that one of us only thought of something, and the other spoke of it. What rare and good fortune, I reflected, to find even one such friend in a lifetme."

In view of this strong expression of mutual understanding, Brother Anandamoy was invited to give his account of the matter. This he preferred not to do. The Brother, who is a quiet and saintly man, did speak of two things. He indicated his feeling that Kriyananda had started a rival organization to the Fellowship, and he expressed his objection to the fact that Kriyananda had taught the Hong Sau technique of concentration in his lesson series *Fourteen Steps to Perfect Joy.*

Since the members of Ananda are *in toto* also members of the SRF, and since a thorough study of the SRF lessons is required for Kriya initiation there, it is difficult to construe the community as a rival organization. It is more properly regarded as a supplementary one.

The Hong Sau technique of concentration, which is given in the SRF lessons twenty-three and twenty-three-A, has also been frequently published elsewhere. It is widely known in India, Japan and in other areas where meditation is extensively practiced. It is not a secret technique, such as the Kriya, and is available to anyone who desires it.

Regardless of the exact circumstances that prevailed at the time, Kriyananda's life forcefully entered a new phase when he departed from the Fellowship. Since he had no desire to enter any other kind of life's work, he necessarily continued on alone as a teacher of yoga and of the principles he had learned from Yogananda. Clearly the demand that he renounce his discipleship and abandon his guru was unreasonable and he did not observe it.

For some five years he carried on as best he could with his

thoughts often fixed on the idea of retreating to some sanctified place to live out his life in silent devotion. Although according to Brother Anandamoy he should have abandoned his spiritual name, and his monkhood, at the time of his dismissal, he retained both. Late in 1980, in an interview granted by Daya Mata to the author, that great lady indicated that this met with her approval. On the same occasion she most graciously accepted an invitation, as Paramhansa Yogananda's greatest living disciple, to dedicate the new temple and World Brotherhood Center at Ananda that had been built in his honor.

The founding of Ananda marked the beginning of the latest, and most significant, phase of Kriyananda's career. It realized his dream and also in part fulfilled Yogananda's call for the establishment of world brotherhood centers dedicated to "plain living and high thinking." Despite the period of cascading domes, once he had started to make Ananda a reality, nothing deterred Kriyananda from his high purpose. It was his teachings that created the devotees who populate it and it is his spiritual guidance that has kept it steadily on the track as a yogic community dedicated to God.

To a lesser man the Ananda of the early eighties might present the opportunity for considerable self gratification and personal power. Kriyananda has steadfastly avoided the first, at least in appearance, and the latter in fact. He is the chairman of the village council, but he has never attended a meeting. His official position is spiritual director; the direct day-to-day administration of Ananda he has long ago delegated to such competent people as Jyotish and Seva. It is his consistent policy to spread the authority for the conduct of Ananda's affairs as broadly as practical; he will not have any part of one-man rule.

At the same time a realistic view must acknowledge that his position at Ananda is unchallengeable. To paraphrase a popular song, whatever swami wants, swami gets, but he is seldom demanding and the things tendered to him are genuine gifts of love. Occasionally, when specific problems arise, he is consulted and invariably his decision is final. He is a good

administrator, but one who does not want to involve himself in
the general operation of the community. That this position is a
wise one is demonstrated frequently when he is away from
Ananda for months at a time. Since a number of Ananda
members are now formally ordained ministers, all the spiritual
services continue uninterrupted with one exception: to date
Kriyananda has not authorized anyone on the ministerial staff
to give Kriya initiation. If he is not present, there is no
initiation until he returns. Since this is an event that normally
takes place only twice a year, the omission is not great.

The home in which he lives is, as stated, a dome. It is large
and sturdy and stands on the edge of a high bluff overlooking
the Yuba River a thousand feet below. From the decking built
in front, there is a spectacular view of space, water and vast
areas of national forest. For a man who sought communion
with nature in her various forms, the location of his home is a
splendid fulfillment.

It is at Ayodhya, the monastic area which is slightly
separated from the main property of Ananda. The atmosphere
is one of exceptional quiet and peace. Very early in the morning
a gentle gong summons the members of the Friends of God to
meditation and prayer, but there are few other interruptions to
the steady forest quiet. Whenever Kriyananda desires to go
into seclusion, which is frequently, he has an almost ideal
residence for the purpose.

On entering the dome the visitor finds himself in a small
foyer off which there is a convenient and comfortable kitchen
that is equipped to prepare food for a small banquet. Down a
few steps is the main floor of the living room with the ceiling
arcing high overhead. Here there are comfortable chairs, a
piano that is kept in tune, and an area that has been set aside
for dining. A beautifully carved Indian screen serves as a room
divider. There are steps to a small balcony where there is a
compact room for the use of infrequent houseguests. Below it
there is a fully equipped bathroom that is an unusual
convenience at Ananda.

There is a lower level in the dome which comprises
Kriyananda's private quarters. They are adequate and

comfortable, but not overly elaborate. They occupy approximately half of the area covered by the main dome; the hillside location makes any extension impractical. The most distinctive feature of the swami's private retreat is a carefuly isolated meditation room where the deep blue color of the walls contributes to an atmosphere for total introspection. Kriyananda frequently remains in this room for hours on end; at such a time only in an extreme emergency would he be disturbed.

A recent wing added at the side of the main dome contains a small recording studio with a control room, and the swami's office. Many a corporation president would like to have one to match it. It is not pretentious, but it is ample in size, roughly octagonal, and from its window there is an inspiring view. It is equipped with a suitable desk, bookcases around most of the circumference, a wood-burning stove for heat, and an up-to-date word processor that the swami finds invaluable for his writing.

Kriyananda's home is frequently used for satsang—a gathering of invited guests for communication and friendship. Dinner invitations are frequent except during the times he is in seclusion. On such occasions the only persons who see him are Keshava, his personal secretary, and the ladies who come in to prepare his meals. The ordinary housekeeping chores are gladly done for him by various members of the community, but if anything substantial in construction or repair is required, he is careful to pay for the work out of his personal funds.

From its inception Ananda has met all of its bills honorably, but any excess monies have been utilized for priority improvements. The coffers of the community have been substantially aided by Kriyananda, especially during the period when he was almost its only financial support. At one time when repairs became urgent and various members of the community were asked for pledges to improve the grounds, those who could promised what they were able, but none were in a position to offer any large amounts. With no visible way to raise the money, Kriyananda secretly pledged $3,000 to improve the roads. Characteristically, he asked his guru for help. Some days later he once again received an unexpected donation that made it possible for him to meet his pledge on time.

Whenever someone is visible to the public as the head of a unique religious organization, the question usually arises as to the sources and extent of his personal income—often with justification. In Kriyananda's case, it is quite possible that the wolf has become excessively tired from waiting at the door. The swami lives comfortably but in anything but a costly manner. His home is heated by wood stoves. Since he is a vegetarian, much of his food comes from the Ananda gardens and little needs to be purchased. His home is unencumbered and he lives, therefore, rent free. His wardrobe, while adequate, is neither extensive nor notably fashionable.

Up until 1981 Kriyananda derived his income basically from three sources. The first is the royalties from his books and from the sale of some of his photographs of Hawaii which have proved popular. (Ananda Publications has them for sale if you are interested.) Secondly, he receives occasional donations from people who specifically ask him to apply the funds to his own use. Thirdly, almost everyone at Ananda tithes as do the community-based businesses. These funds go to the Ananda Cooperative Village treasury and to the Yoga Fellowship. These two organizations, in turn tithe from these amounts for the support of their spiritual leader.

In 1981 it was realized that during the years of Ananda's existence Kriyananda had put some very substantial sums into the treasury, but had never taken anything whatever out except for the limited tithes intended to meet his minimal requirements. In 1981 the community voted to offer him a salary. Up to that time he had been drawing a 3% royalty on his books, nothing whatever on his tapes. Many gifts presented to him personally he in turn had passed on to either Ananda or the Yoga Fellowship, whichever was indicated. He has never displayed any ambition to become personally affluent.

One of the ingredients that has made Kriyananda so immensely popular with the Ananda population is his informality. At one time a member of the community had just finished painting the floor of the old farmhouse, which is now Master's Market. Kriyananda was about to preside at a formal ceremony, and had dressed for the occasion, when he received a phone call. The phone was located on the second floor of the building and the wet paint made it impossible for him to get in that way. In full robes he went up a construction ladder and in through the window. Observed the painter, "Nothing stops a yogi."

He is also tolerant of lapses from grace providing they are relatively innocent and not repeated. There is a strict anti-alcohol rule at Ananda, but this did not preclude one member from returning home from Nevada City definitely loaded. It was also his misfortune to encounter the swami while in that condition. Recognizing that everyone is entitled to an occasional moment of rebellion, Kriyananda said nothing about it and took no action. The occasion did not reoccur.

One of the most agreeable aspects of Kriyananda is his sense of humor. He is a great fan of P.G. Wodehouse and has a large collection of Wodehousiana in his home. Often to illustrate a point he will tell a story. One of his favorites concerns a veteran policeman, aged fifty-four, who hauled a ninety-year-old pensioner into court for disorderly conduct and resisting arrest. When the court asked the defendant for an explanation of his conduct in fighting the officer, he declared that he wasn't going to have any runny nosed kid telling *him* what to do.

Kriyananda sings very well and he enjoys being invited to do so. He is not reluctant to be the center of attention when meetings are held at his home, which is a role he could not escape if he tried. By reasonable and civilized standards, he is entitled to it. For Ananda is his vindication: his carrying on of his guru's work after he had been banished, stripped of his credentials as a disciple, and subjected to great personal humiliation which, in fair appraisal, he did not deserve.

Pain inflicted for misdeeds can be most uncomfortable: that which is inflicted undeservedly can be far more acute. Even if he had indeed exceeded his authority in India, he had gone about the Self Realization Fellowship's business with great zeal and when he had run into official obstructionism, he went first to Indira Ghandi, and later to her father, Nehru, and successfully enlisted their help. He was definitely an original and he paid the price for it. The same might be said of many thousands of gifted men and women throughout history who were victimized because of their exceptional abilities.

Whatever motivated Tara to take the drastic action she took, quite obviously she did not take into consideration the well-known principle that you do not penalize someone who is doing his or her best to aid your cause.

It is entirely possible that in dismissing Kriyananda the Self Realization Fellowship may have had other grounds which have not been made public. If so, no visible evidence has ever emerged. It is known that several other devotees clashed with Tara and left the Fellowship as a consequence. Whatever the precise circumstances, Kriyananda was subjected to such a severe emotional and spiritual trauma that in almost twenty years he has not been able to free himself from its disastrous effects. He keeps it well hidden deep within himself, but if he at times seems to take more than usual satisfaction in what he has accomplished, there are few who would deny that he has grounds for justification.

The question has arisen in many minds as to what would happen to Ananda if for any reason Kriyananda were unable to continue as its leading resident and spiritual director. There is no one in the community who even approaches his charisma, and no possible replacement is in sight. It is the consensus that the community would continue, most probably under the direction of John Novak, but it would never be the same. There is a long-standing member of the SRF who offered the opinion that when Kriyananda left, the Fellowship lost its most brilliant rising leader. Subsequent events tend to support this opinion, though it must be noted that the very strict rules imposed by the SRF on its renunciate members may well be hiding some outstanding talent within its ranks.

Kriyananda today is in a position to live very much as he chooses, discounting those life styles that call for excessive spending. He writes extensively and whatever he produces is guaranteed publication without that bane of authorship: excessive editorial interference with his thoughts and ideas. He is very open to constructive comments and if they strike him as valid, he acts on them. When it was remarked to him that it might be a sound idea to produce a consensed version of *The Path*, updated to include the Ananda story, he weighed the thought and then spent weeks in preparing a new manuscript. Although the original version had won the praise of thousands, in the paperback edition the reader is faced with some 650 pages of very small type. In the new and shorter version the meat of the original is retained while the whole has been updated to include much about Ananda that did not appear in the original.

During most of his adult lifetime, Yogananda wore long hair, well before the advent of rock bands and others who followed this practice. There is a belief among yogis that long hair in a certain way increases the sensitivity of the subject to supernatural vibrations. During Spiritual Renewal Week in 1980 he appeared one day with his hair cut. It seemed to be the consensus of Ananda members that he looked better with short hair and that his new image would enable him to travel when he so desired as Donald Walters without revealing his monastic standing. He wears his beard neatly trimmed so that he would appear to almost any sophisticated layman as a successful doctor, stockbroker, or as a member of almost any profession.

Conversation with him is always stimulating, particularly in view of the fact that he can discourse with authority on a wide variety of topics. But the one dearest to his heart is Ananda and the yogic teachings that brought it into being. His dedication to his chosen Path is total and when he was once asked if he had ever considered marrying and raising a family, he replied, "I have never felt the lack."

At the same time he is generous in releasing renunciates from their vows if he is convinced that it would be in the best interests of their lives and spiritual development. Shivani was once a nun, but when it became clear that she and Arjuna were falling very much in love and would like to be married, he released her and gave his blessing to their union.

Early in 1981 he made himself available for an all-day interview that covered a wide range of ideas, most of which were concerned with Ananda. In speaking of the community he said:

> In this age of competition Ananda can demonstrate that it is not necessary to cut others down to build one's self up. In a community of one thousand business men each man has nine hundred and ninety-nine rivals. But if we work together, we can have nine hundred and ninety-nine friends. Ananda believes that to cooperate with people is more important than to fight with them. At Ananda we can turn from the world and cooperate with nature: seeking not what is right for just one, but what is right for everyone. A loss one time can be a gain in the long run when benefit for others comes first. The Ananda fire was an example of this.

Later he remarked:

> The great problem of our age is alienation. Most of us don't know our own neighbors, or we know them to speak to, not to cry with. It is necessary to break the little bond of I and Mine. It is instinctive to people at Ananda that other people everywhere are still our own.
>
> In our age we subscribe to the idea that the government must take care of people, but Ananda shows that a community can take care of its own people. We don't need government handouts; with will and love people can take care of their own. Politically, socially and economically this is most important, showing that spiritually the small community can serve in these areas. At Ananda this is a step forward related to America's very traditions. We don't need to step backward; we can pick up the pieces of America's traditions that have been forgotten and tie them in with the future.

In discussing the structure of Ananda, he said:

> We're not doing this only for ourselves, we're doing it for the sake of all the people to come. God has always forced service upon us. One of the ways that He forced it upon us was that mortgage; if we hadn't had to pay two thousand dollars a month, Ananda would be a very different place today. We were forced to reach out to other people instead of just living peacefully and quietly here. Our kind of spiritual energy is needed by the world. We are here to do what God wants to do through us.

He also added two comments that seemed in particular to typify the kind of spiritual guidance that he provides for the rapidly expanding Ananda membership. "It's easy to be open-minded," he said, "on a subject in which you have no serious interest."

In defining the spiritual life and what objectives might be achieved through it, he offered a significant comment: "God won't do it for you, but He will do it with you if you do your best."

As a swami, Kriyananda has almost alone created a new image for one aspect of that ancient order. Despite his still ingrained love of solitude and seclusion, he is very approachable and outgoing under most circumstances. He is a delightful host and despite his celibate status, he has a very definite appeal to women who find his company most agreeable even though he is clearly unavailable.

Despite this aspect of his character, he sometimes chooses to keep the reasons for some of his actions strictly within himself. There are topics he declines to discuss, most often those related to spiritual decisions he has taken and which are normally not subject to appeal. When asked about something, he often responds by saying, "I didn't feel guided to do that." It is widely known within the SRF that Yogananda appeared after his *mahasamadhi* (earthly death) to Daya Mata and also to his devoted disciple James Lynn. If he has ever done so to Kriyananda, the swami will not speak of it. If the topic is brought up, he dismisses it as soon as possible. He is also totally reluctant to discuss any communication he may have had with his guru through prayer, despite the fact that many have reported such experiences.

In the position which he now occupies, Kriyananda could well, and easily, accept the status of guru—something that has been offered to him on many occasions. He has been totally steadfast in his refusal. When one very sincere devotee relatively new to the Path wrote to him and asked that he be her guru, he replied that Yogananda was her guru, but that he would be glad to serve as a teacher if so desired. Beyond this point he will not go.

Kriyananda's strongest abilities as a spiritual leader lie in teaching and public lectures. At one time he was less comfortable as a pastor or personal counselor, but he has been known to take a great deal of time to assist someone with a spiritual problem and he listens with total concentration if the occasion requires. Many times he has offered his advice in the form of a single sentence rather than in any extended discourse, but those who have sought his help have very often found his brief answers precisely what they sought. Once he told someone who wanted to consult him, "Why don't you wait six months and then come and see me." When the petitioner said that such a delay would be intolerable, Kriyananda took the whole of the next morning to help him solve his problem.

It has been often said that no man is a hero to his valet. This may well be true simply because there are so few valets left in the world, but one very notable thing about Kriyananda is that those who know him best, and have been with him for the longest period of time, are his most loyal and dedicated supporters. Considering the fact that 85% of the Ananda residents have been to college, and that many have been admitted to advanced degrees, this is not the reaction of the great unwashed. It is a solemn judgment by capable and intelligent people who live with him on a day to day basis.

He does not extract their respect and devotion; it is given freely and by the wish of the donors. He does not seek popularity and he has been known to make decisions that were certain to be unpopular. Nevertheless he made them and they were accepted as his wish and will. It is very strongly felt at Ananda that he is being directly guided by the guru they have not met nor seen. Kriyananda never speaks of this or makes any claim, even by indirection, except to comment upon occasion that he did not feel guided to take a certain action.

One thing, however, is certain: he has made his mark as a disciple of his guru and it is one that time may see grow to prime importance.

Chapter Seventeen

India Faire—Renjyuin

When spring comes to northern California and growing things begin to sprout in the ground, the people of Ananda become much more visible at The Farm and at the Meditation Retreat. The garden gopis, as they like to call themselves, are seen hard at work; many other people are busy planting flowers, raking gravel, painting and doing other things to beautify the grounds. They eat their lunches in the out-of-doors and sit silently at twilight in meditation. With the end of winter, activities seem to pick up everywhere. And the spirit of joy, which is so much a part of Ananda, becomes more manifest.

At this time the parade of visitors to the community considerably increases. Newcomers arrive to take part in the apprentice program; and the Meditation Retreat fills to capacity. Casual visitors drop by to see Ananda, while the families of members often come for longer visits. The telephone switchboard is constantly busy and the air is filled with the sounds of construction, blacksmithing and schoolchildren. Near Master's Market the tantalizing aroma of freshly baked bread suggests the good things to eat that are being made ready.

Many of the people who come to visit Ananda ask the same questions: where do all these people come from? And soon after that: what has caused them to take up this manner of living?

Sociologists and other students of human behavior have pointed out that if a society be founded, no matter how outlandish, some people will be found to join it. Whenever some prophet proclaims the end of the world, and is reckless enough to name the date, hundreds will often turn out to keep vigil with

him, ready to meet the angel Gabriel. And in England there is a
going organization known as the Flat Earth Society. Therefore
it can be understood why some who have never seen Ananda,
or met any members of its spiritual family, tend to believe that
the community is populated by a collection of dropouts, drifters
and, to utilize the now accepted term, Jesus Freaks.

This is somewhat akin to suggesting that the Southern
Baptist Convention is largely made up of the Sexual Freedom
League.

The population of Ananda is remarkably stable. The
average tenure is currently much more than ten years.
Collectively the members represent an astonishingly wide
background in terms of both occupation and experience. The
1980 Ananda census asked the question: what was your job just
before coming to Ananda? Here are some of the answers:

attorney	immigration director
music teacher	editor
secretary	yoga teacher
nurse	domestic
taxi driver	photographer
carpenter	engineer
marketing analyst	interior designer
massage therapist	postal carrier
teacher	logger
woodworker	accountant
painter	research assistant
manager, import business	cook
actor	machinist
hospital lab technician	tax auditor
office manager	camp counselor
bookkeeper	baker
musician	banker
landscape designer	librarian
occupational therapist	policeman
home remodeler	caterer
college professor	dental assistant
naturalist	medical student
farm equipment builder	special education teacher
laborer	nurseryman
steel contractor	social worker

Another question asked was: what is your present age (in
this incarnation)? The answers ranged from eighteen to sixty-

nine with a distribution equivalent to the national population as a whole. When asked where they had received their higher education, the Ananda members came up with a long list of accredited institutions ranging from Bethany Bible College to the London School of Cordon Bleu (yes, there is a Cordon Bleu chef at Ananda).

It is interesting that in response to the question: during your years at home were your parents married, divorced or separated, 87% reported that their parents were married. Only 7% considered that their family income during their childhood was below average; 39% considered their families to have been above average or wealthy.

Very significant are the answers to three religious questions:

What religion were you born into? This evoked a wide response from Roman Catholic (27%) to Islam (1%).

Were you raised (educated) in that religion? Yes, 80%.

Did you at some point question or reject those teachings? Yes, 85%.

The favorite magazine at Ananda is the *National Geographic. Time, Newsweek* and the *Mother Earth News* are runners up.

From the above data it can be seen that the people of Ananda come from solid, substantial homes, are well educated, had religious upbringings, and represented a wide spectrum of professions and occupations before deciding to join the community as active resident members. Once at Ananda all differences of background and economic status tend to evaporate in the common dedication to God and to the teachings of Paramhansa Yogananda. As someone remarked, "Living in a spiritual family like this is great. For one thing, you can talk about reincarnation if you want to without having to look around first to be sure there isn't a Catholic nearby."

The Ananda census includes many data on how the present members first heard about the community, how they came to visit, and what specifically called them onto the Path. But the data by themselves are sterile and sometimes unintentionally misleading.

Many New Age religious organizations, according to the media, appear to be made up of semi-brainwashed young people who have been caught up in a born-again frenzy or who have been captured by a charismatic prophet of some kind. This is not even remotely true of Ananda. The people of the community came there because they chose to do so; they stay because the life that it offers, with all of its limitations, is for them far more rewarding than any other. And in their guru they have found a strong guiding light, despite the fact that not one of them ever knew him during his lifetime, Kriyananda excepted.

Because Yogananda came from India, the community has a strong affinity for that nation. Many of the residents have been there and others are saving to go. Indian banquets are often served to mark special occasions and the harmonium, which is widely used in India, is played by almost everyone. Also, each midsummer Ananda stages an Indian Faire. It is a gala occasion with booths, fortune-tellers, wandering sadhus (story tellers), Indian dancers, Indian food and Indian music to enliven the occasion. The Faire is held at the Retreat and despite the relatively remote location, it normally draws a considerable crowd. Everyone has a good time sampling the food, watching the archery contest, seeing the exhibition of Indian art, enjoying the intricate Indian dances, and going on the pilgrimage. This is a fanciful tour set up through the forest during which the "devotees" are taken to see various sights of India. Each tour is accompanied by a guide who explains many things, including how certain demons lurk under tiny bridges and how safe passage can be secured by saying a little prayer while walking across. There are many other features.

The magic of Ananda, and the inner feelings it can generate, may be found in the story of a certain lady who came with her husband to the Faire and who there had a remarkable experience neither she nor anyone else had even remotely expected.

It is necessary to know a little about her background. Her parents came to the New World from Northern Ireland, bringing with them their staunch Protestant faith. An only child, she was raised in the tenets of the Episcopalian Church and absorbed them naturally. When she was married, her church unrolled its finest carpeting and vestments because she was one of their own and they recognized all of the work she had already done for them.

Later, so that she might share her husband's faith, she became a Lutheran, but kept to her steady churchgoing, attendance at communion, and Bible reading every night before retiring. She had found her religious life and in it she was fully satisfied and happy.

After she had been married many years, one day a Japanese friend came to call. This lady had been quite substantially built, but when the door was opened to her, she stood waiting neat, trim, and beaming a wide smile. During the tea chatter that followed, the Japanese lady told her secret— she had been taking yoga lessons. The yoga teacher, a Japanese master of great repute, had brought about a remarkable change. She had lost forty pounds. Furthermore, the constant shots she had had to take were no longer necessary; she was glowing with health and had more vitality than ever before in her adult life. Then the Japanese lady came to the point: the yoga master needed a new place to teach. It would be greatly appreciated if he could use the house they were in on Saturday mornings.

That presented certain problems, but refusal would have been difficult. The following Saturday morning the class, which was composed almost entirely of nubile and flexible young women, came to its new meeting place and the hostess, under some pressure, joined the group. She hadn't the remotest concept of yoga, but she did know the importance of caring for her body. With the others she began to bend and to flex some of her muscles that hadn't been used in that manner since, as a young woman, she had been a dancer.

Some four years later, at the conclusion of the class, there was a brief ceremony. The master donned a formal robe, rang a small chime, and called her before him. When she was seated in the lotus posture, he read from a scroll, tapped her gently with a fan, and bestowed upon her the *shodan* degree. In the martial arts, this is the first level of the black belt. He also did more: in recognition of her superior achievement, and following the Japanese custom, he awarded to her the name Renjyuin, which translates, "The Lady of the Lotus." The new shodan placed her palms together and bowed her formal acceptance and thanks. She had learned much and had learned it extremely well, but her instruction had been confined to hatha yoga: the many postures, the technique of *shiatsu* (acupressure), and yogic body alignment. Very little had been said about meditation and nothing whatever about the spiritual aspect of yoga, despite the fact that the teacher was a Buddhist priest.

The yoga had added a great deal to her life, and had given her back the body of a young woman, but it had not in any way influenced her deep religious dedication. It never occurred to her that it ever would. Particularly on the days on which she took communion, she felt richly satisfied. With her husband she had traveled extensively around and throughout the world, but none of the many different kinds and houses of worship were to her anything more than interesting tourist attractions. She spent some time in India, but was not attracted by the country despite the fact that she liked many of the people she met there.

In 1978 she entertained two houseguests from England, distinguished persons who were professional associates of her husband. Since the British visitors were most anxious to see something of the West, arrangements were made to rent a large motor home for a tour. Then the gentleman expressed a wish: he would like to see an American ashram.

Renjyuin knew of none, nor did her husband, but he made inquiries. He learned of a place called Ananda and discovered that it was not too far off the route that had already been projected. He made a private call to the community to ask if visitors were welcome. He was told that they definitely were and was given directions.

Two weeks later, on a Saturday night and in a pouring rain, their motor home pulled into Nevada City, gassed up, and they obtained local directions to Ananda. An hour later, far out in the country, it had become clear to everyone that they were

on the wrong road. It took another hour to get back to Nevada
City. At that point, the time being very late, the British guests
strongly urged that the program be abandoned. There was a
schedule to be kept and little time remained to see the ashram.
But Renjyuin's husband was not one to give up; he obtained
fresh directions and set off once more. Something around two
in the morning he pulled into the small parking lot in front of
the Apprentice Village.

In the morning the weather was glorious. A young woman
came to the motor home to invite everyone to breakfast, but
they had already eaten. She then suggested that they might
like to see the Meditation Retreat where the Sunday service
would be held. Since the British gentleman was most
interested, with the young lady as guide the motor home was
piloted over the difficult fire access road and up the hill where
there was just barely room to clear the trees on each side, and
parked near to the temple.

The guide informed the party that the service would begin
shortly and invited everyone to attend. The British lady
declined; she was not feeling well and wanted to rest. The
British gentleman was anxious to go and his host agreed to
accompany him. Then he turned toward his wife, asking her to
come too.

She would have none of it. She had been uncomfortable
from the moment the motor home had driven onto the grounds;
a religious community of an unusual kind conflicted sharply
with her own views. Furthermore, she was not about to enter an
unknown temple where she might be compelled to bow down
and worship false gods. Heathen Indian deities were not for
her. She would remain in the motor home and keep the other
lady company.

With his British guest the husband went to the service in
the dome-shaped temple. The congregation gathered and sat
quietly, some on the floor by preference, some on the few rows
of benches provided in the back. Green living plants decorated
the front of the temple and to one side a statue of Christ held out
its hands in blessing.

Presently a young man came in carrying a guitar. He

seated himself on a small platform, plucked a few chords, and started a simple hymn. The congregation sang, not in the mumbling manner of many such assemblies, but with clarity and a knowledge of the words and melody. A second chant followed, then a third. After that, there was a brief period of meditation. "Think of the past week," the young minister said, "think of the blessings you have received from God, then offer Him your thanks."

Renjyuin's husband sat silently, experiencing something he had never before found in any church he had attended. There had been no ritual, no standing up and sitting down, no recitations of introits and collects which held very little meaning for him, no droning on of long litany. Instead there was simple and direct worship of God. He studied the altar painting that displayed six pictures. Jesus, taken from the famous Hoffman conception, was instantly recognizable, but he did not understand the young man sitting with his eyes cast heavenward, nor the older man with a grizzled mustache and his eyes tight shut. This, however, was only a minor distraction. When the young minister began to speak, he listened.

The sermon was short, hardly more than ten minutes, and delivered in a very quiet, informal style that gave meaning to the words. And as he listened the man who had come as a courtesy to his guest began to feel something stir within him. This was the kind of church service he had always hoped to attend. When the brief sermon was over and the singing began once more, he wished that he could have joined in. And when the service concluded, he responded to the way that people greeted him. They were the kind of people he understood and their pleasant welcome without effusion gave him a warm lift. If this was Ananda, he was for it. But more than that, within that spherical temple he had experienced something that reached deep within his being.

He spoke to the minister and invited him to come to the motor home for a cup of coffee; he wanted Renjyuin to meet him and realized how much he wished that she might have been at the service. The minister accepted and stopped in for a very few minutes. He said that his name was Nitai and Renjyuin was polite to him.

In February the husband returned to Ananda and spent a week participating in a retreat program. When he returned home, he brought back with him the *Fourteen Steps to Perfect Joy,* Kriyananda's tape series on *How to Meditate,* and some other material. His wife was not especially interested, but she greeted him warmly and was glad to have him with her once more.

As the spring came, and then the summer, the husband spent much time with the *Fourteen Steps.* He also read *The Path* and *Autobiography of a Yogi.*

Twice Kriyananda and a few Ananda members who were traveling with him came for dinner. Renjyuin had to contend with a vegetarian menu, something totally new to her, but she managed brilliantly. By the accounts of those present, she provided gourmet dinners. By her statement she was nervous about Kriyananda; she had never met a swami before and was uncertain what he represented. But when, after dinner, he produced his guitar and sang for her, she was very pleased. The evenings went very well indeed.

In July a business trip took Renjyuin's husband to the Pacific Northwest. To make a small vacation of it, she went along to keep him company. When, on the way back, he proposed that they stop by at Ananda, her attitude had softened enough for her to say that if he wanted to go, she was willing to go with him.

Thus it was, by coincidence, that they came to India Faire. They had not known that it would be on, but since they arrived the day before, they planned to attend. That Sunday morning Renjyuin did go to the Sunday Service and came out of the temple with the feeling that she had indeed been to church.

At the Faire they had lunch and spent much of the afternoon watching the various events. Renjyuin particularly enjoyed the obviously fine art of an Indian dancer, and she no longer felt uncomfortable on the Ananda grounds. She had met some of the people around her and she had liked them very much. They had a certain warmth she could not help but admire. But some of the Indian food did not appeal to her.

They had seen almost all of the Faire and Renjyuin had looked at her watch several times. It would be a long drive back to southern California and she was becoming anxious to get started. She had many things to do at home and had been away for some time. At that point her husband bought tickets to go on the pilgrimage. Long accustomed to the fact that he was constantly leading her into activities that were not of her choosing, she patiently agreed to tag along.

She enjoyed it. Several of the exhibits were fun things and she laughed along with the rest. She was not required to bow down to anyone and the obvious spirit of the whole event was light hearted. Then the guide, the "ancient devotee," who was an accomplished actress of thirty at the most, led her party into a little forest grove and the mood changed abruptly.

Seated in a tree was a young woman softly playing an autoharp. There was a small open area of very green grass; seated in regal splendor was a young man painted all over in black, and holding the three-pronged spear of Shiva. As Renjyuin sat on a stump to rest, one by one the Ananda members who were on the little tour went forward, knelt before Shiva, and received his blessing. It was quiet and lovely in the still of the forest. And then the miracle happened.

Let it be told in Renjyuin's own words:

> One of the India Faire's features was a pretend pilgrimage led by an 'ancient devotee,' all fun and games until we reached the shrine of Shiva. There in a beautiful wooded spot we all gathered before a young man painted black, carrying a three-pronged spear of Shiva (the epitome of all I disliked and equated with heathen deities) and a lovely girl in a tree playing a harp. As part of the Pilgrimage, people were primed (Ananda people) to go up and receive Shiva's blessing, which they did. But then a strange thing happened—whether it was the peace, the beauty of the place, the other world calm of the moment, I found myself stumbling off my tree stump and going to Shiva for a blessing—a touch of his black finger against my forehead.
>
> I will never forget that moment. I sat feeling just joy and peace as I watched every member of the group do as I had done. That was my first step on the Path; Shiva wasn't a black heathen god, he was reverence, beauty, peace, calm, acceptance of all life: for just that moment I was able to see beyond symbols into reality.

Upon her return home, Renjyuin began to meditate. She studied the *Fourteen Steps*, listened to the tapes many times, and began to buy other writings of Yogananda from Ananda and the Self Realization Fellowship. She would often disappear during the day, sitting alone in the little meditation room she had prepared in a corner of a closet. She still continued her regular church attendance, but in addition she read Yogananda, Kriyananda, and the lives of the yoga masters.

Renjyuin received Kriya initiation at the end of Spiritual Renewal Week held during August 1980. Because she had already been given a spiritual name, Kriyananda asked that she keep it; she is now Renjyuin to everyone at Ananda. She is the only Ananda member with a Japanese name, but Ananda has learned both to spell and pronounce it. She is a deeply dedicated follower of her guru, Paramhansa Yogananda, and devotes two to three hours of each day to her studies, meditation and practice of the yoga postures.

Many have come before her, many will undoubtedly come after, but to her, when she sat once more within the temple and received the gift of the Kriya, the doors of the heaven she had always aspired to were opened and a new life, founded in unlimited joy and happiness, lay waiting before her.

Chapter Eighteen

Ananda, California—The City

By the time Ananda had completed its first decade, and the end of the 1970s began to come into sight, it was abundantly clear that the community was a notable success. It had weathered reverses that no one would have expected it to survive and, like the Phoenix, it had arisen stronger each time. It still had not accumulated significant financial reserves, but communities are not judged by cash alone. In particular Ananda had acquired a priceless asset that continued to appreciate solidly, its people.

In the very beginning, the doors were open to almost anyone who professed an interest in the yogic way of life and who also was ready to take up a rural life style in a community environment. Within a short time it had become evident that this was not the way to build a solid structure. From that time forward admission to Ananda became far more selective. There are no ethnic or religious barriers other than the requirement that the potential residents be disciples of Paramhansa Yogananda and that they follow the yogic path. Since this policy was adopted, Ananda has continued to grow steadily. Those who have come and have stayed are clearly "Ananda people," of the kind that are genuinely wanted and who are well equipped to fit into the life of the community.

The key to Ananda's success has been described by Devi Novak and others as "personal transformation." Few of the people who apply to the community are ready at once to join in its life and activities as fully dedicated members and devotees of Yogananda, but this orientation usually comes with a little time. Some who come with the most serious intentions discover that they are not ready to take up Ananda's life style and

223

decide to leave.

There are four classes of membership at Ananda. They have been established for some time and experience has shown that the organizational structure is a good one.

The first level of membership, once known as the Circle of Joy, is now more appropriately called the Ananda Spiritual Family. It is open to any interested individuals who would like to be part of the community even if only in an indirect way. They may reside anywhere and in any country. In exchange for moderate dues, members of the Spiritual Family regularly receive various publications produced for them, such as *The Practice of Joy Newsletter*, the *Joy Circular*, and, in addition, announcements of news and events at the community. They are encouraged to have a "pen pal" relationship with full-time Ananda residents, which the Spiritual Family office will be glad to arrange. On Wednesday evenings the community invites members of the Family, or any others who are interested, to phone Ananda with requests for prayers, spiritual advice, or just a chat. A member of the ministerial staff will be on hand to take the incoming calls. The number is (916) 265-5877.

Members of the Spiritual Family are encouraged to visit Ananda whenever they can; their welcome is assured. Whenever Ananda personnel are in their vicinity, if practical a satsang will be held so that members may come to know one another and also the members from Ananda proper. Finally, members of the Spiritual Family receive a discount on all Ananda publications, recordings and other material.

The Spiritual Family lives up to its name, since it also includes all Ananda members of whatever level. By 1982 the total had passed 1000 and was continuing to grow rapidly.

The second level of membership is made up of those who have chosen to come to Ananda to live and who are in a probationary period. This probation extends in both directions: it is a time for getting acquainted, for adjusting to Ananda's life style and ideals, and to the many activities that are constantly going on. Both the community and the newcomers have the opportunity to evaluate each other and, perhaps, to make adjustments as they may be indicated. There is no set time for this; it may be only a few weeks or it can extend over several months.

By this time the new individual, couple or family will know whether or not Ananda is for them a permanent home and life style. If it isn't, then there are no hard feelings if they choose to withdraw. Some have done so only to come back a year later with the firm declaration that this time it is for keeps. And almost always it is.

When by mutual consent the time has come, the provisional members will come up for the vote of the membership committee and of the community at large. Unless objections have been filed, this is usually only a formality in the form of a recognition and welcoming ceremony.

When the provisional members have passed through this process they advance to the third level as full members of Ananda. This includes permanent residency privileges, but there are many full members of Ananda who do not reside within the community. There are quite a few in Nevada City and many other localities. By this time the new members will have paid their membership fees or, if not able to do so, will have made arrangements for payment at a later date. The majority of the residential members of Ananda belong to this level.

The fourth and final level comprise the members of the Yoga Fellowship. The qualification here is clear-cut: to become one of this "inner circle," the candidate must have been a full member of Ananda for five years. In this group are the core personnel and those who, through their service, have earned the right to join with them.

Although these different levels exist, they are in no way evident in the day to day life of Ananda or in the relationships between the resident members. Often relative newcomers become very popular and are assigned to responsible jobs. There is no way to distinguish between a provisional resident and a member of the Yoga Fellowship. Snobbery of any kind is unknown; there isn't even a whiff of it at Ananda. If there is a distinction at all, it is between those who have achieved Kriya initiation and those who aspire to it. The happy fact is that the members of the first group do all they can to help the as yet uninitiated to achieve their goal.

The purpose of the Yoga Fellowship is to guarantee that important policy decisions concerning the community will be made by those whose judgment and dedication have been thoroughly established, and who have had extended experience in the Ananda environment.

By the late 1970s Ananda began to expand its rate of growth. The most important single step was the gift to the community of 908 acres of prime land near the ocean at Occidental, California. This splendid donation was made by Mr. Peter Myers who had had aspirations himself of starting a community on the site. When this proved impractical, he presented the entire property to Ananda. For legal reasons title is being transferred at the rate of 10% per annum, but the community has the full use of all the land. This satellite community has been named Ocean Song.

At present about thirty Ananda members reside at Ocean Song and are gradually developing the property. A branch of the Ananda schools has been started there, a garden and some appropriate cottage industries.

In September 1979 Ananda House was established in San Francisco. Physically it is a splendid forty-five room mansion set in one of the finest residential sections of the city. For some months Kriyananda had been looking into the idea of a San Francisco center, but he had been cautious in making sure that such a facility was really wanted. When the fine old mansion was used as the Decorators' Showcase in 1979, it came to the attention of some Ananda members. They visited it and decided that as a facility it would be almost perfect, but expensive. The rent would be $3,000 per month without the top floor that had a separate entrance. With the top floor it would be $4,500, not including the estimated $13,500 that it would cost to move in.

A meeting was held and within half an hour all of the necessary commitments to make the center possible were received. The property was then leased. Ananda House consists of three main floors and parts of two additional levels below. Fine carved oak and polished marble are much in evidence. At present some thirty members reside in Ananda House and there is a considerable waiting list of those who would like to move in. A former music room on the front of the first floor has been converted into a near ideal temple. In addition there is a large meditation room, an almost equally large area for practicing the asanas (yoga postures) and a comfortable dining room where meals are served.

In addition to the residence, Ananda House operates a teaching facility with many classes given similar to those offered at the Meditation Center. The directors and resident ministers are John (Jyotish) Novak and his wife Devi. Visitors are welcome and are encouraged to come. Free weekly programs and services are offered. When desired, personal counseling, which is of a high calibre, is also available. Ananda House is in Pacific Heights at 2320 Broadway; the telephone is (415) 567-8070.

Other Ananda residential centers have been established in Sacramento, Stockton, Nevada City and on the San Francisco Peninsula in Atherton. All of them have temple facilities and also serve as teaching centers. Since during the first quarter of 1981 two had to move to larger quarters, local inquiry, or a call to Ananda, is recommended prior to a visit. The welcome mat, to coin a platitude, is out at all of them.

All of this expansion activity indicated very clearly that Ananda has reached a stage in its development when it can no longer be regarded as a group of religiously oriented people who live together in the woods. As the mail flow increased still more, and as the list of prospective members continued to expand, Ananda made a momentous decision early in 1980. It decided to apply for incorporation as a municipality.

The plan appeared to make good sense. Ananda had been for some time a successful village and had demonstrated both its stability and the capability to govern itself. It was already larger than many incorporated cities in California. Furthermore, Ananda had called on all its neighbors to ask if they would like to be included in the new municipality. Several indicated that they were in favor of the idea.

Once incorporated, Ananda would be freed from the stiffling burden of red tape that some few members of the Nevada County administration had inflicted on it. Also, and much more important, it would be able to make a much more efficient use of its land and plan a better laid-out community.

In the words of the official Ananda Municipal Incorporation Proposal:

> Ananda has long governed itself successfully to the greatest extent allowable under the law. The community has now reached a level of development and political maturity where it is ready to assume even more direct responsibility for its future growth and direction.

Many of the municipal requirements could be easily met. Police protection was available from the sheriff at a very reasonable cost. Fire protection is not a requirement, but it would be available from the North San Juan Volunteer Fire Department as well as Ananda's own people and equipment. Forest fires would remain the responsibility of the Department of Forestry. Within the ranks of the Ananda members there were many skilled people fully qualified to discharge the necessary administrative functions. It is quite common in California's smaller municipalities for part time and volunteer help to be used.

In preparing its proposal Ananda engaged Mr. William R. Zion, a professional consultant in local and regional government, to prepare an Economic Feasibility Study. This Mr. Zion did and submitted his report on 30 December 1980. It was his professional opinion, based on the pertinent data, that the incorporation was feasible. Even using the most conservative figures, it was clear that Ananda was well prepared to meet its obligations as an incorporated entity.

In order to be sure that the functions of church and state would be entirely separated in the new Ananda, provisions were made in the planning to elect a town council which would replace the County Board of Supervisors in governing the community. The council, in turn, would appoint a planning commission to replace the present county commission. These two political bodies would be entirely separate from the existing village council and the Yoga Fellowship.

As visualized, the incorporated city (or town—which is the same thing in California) would include all of the present Ananda property except for the Meditation Retreat and, in addition, certain properties presently owned by Hebel, Wilson, Delaney and Rabon. These holdings combined equal 1.04 square miles, which happens to be almost exactly the same size, geographically, as Nevada City.

After incorporation, some of the property in the new city would be municipally owned, some privately owned, and some held, for religious purposes, by the Yoga Fellowship. Only the Yoga Fellowship property would continue to enforce the no-alcohol rule; drug abuse would be prohibited as it is now. According to present plans, 93% of the new city would be made up of land now owned by Ananda, the other outside owners contributing the additional 7% of the total. Only a very limited area, as at present, would be tax-free. As of 1981, 97% of the total Ananda land holdings were on the tax rolls; only 3% was tax-free because of being used for religious purposes only.

As soon as the decision was made to go ahead with the incorporation, Ananda called upon two talented ladies to devote virtually their full time to the project. One of these is Miss Dallas Atkins, a member of the California bar. As an attorney, Miss Atkins undertook the legal work that would be required. As the other member of the prime team Ananda called upon one of its prize communications assets—Asha.

During Spiritual Renewal Week in August 1981, Miss Atkins was most diligent in seeing to it that all Ananda adults were properly registered to vote. She prepared all of the necessary documents, saw to it that the forms were properly filled out, and did all of the required filing. Local politicians suddenly became aware of the fact that a *bloc* of several hundred voters was going to take a keen interest in their activities and decisions. This was, the community knew, strictly in the American tradition. It is both a privilege and a duty to vote; the Ananda membership was fully prepared to exercise this precious franchise.

In connection with the incorporation, Asha wrote:

> It should be emphasized that Ananda's desire to incorporate comes not from the thought that the community has been unfairly treated. Rather it is motivated by the simple fact that the complexity of Ananda's development could be more efficiently handled at the very local level. It would also relieve an already overburdened county system. This is precisely what municipal incorporation is designed to accomplish.

She also pointed out that what Ananda is doing today is exactly what many other pioneer communities did a century ago: establish a community, incorporate it, and assume the responsibility for its future welfare.

A small group of people—The San Juan Taxpayers Association—appeared in opposition to the incorporation. A petition was circulated and 182 signatures were obtained, the net result of which was to impose on Ananda the need to prepare still another Environmental Impact Report. It is difficult for an observer to understand how a change in the political structure of a certain area can have any measurable impact on the environment at all, but Ananda accepted the burden and to a degree blamed itself for not having carried out a more effective community relations program which would have made such a petition almost as impossible as the EIR appears unnecessary.

At the time of the Ananda announcement, there were only two incorporated communities in Nevada County: Grass Valley and Nevada City. There is also a community in the county called Truckee which would appear to be a likely candidate for incorporation, but reputedly opposing factions within this area have been unable to agree on the desirability of taking this political step. Ananda, therefore, was called upon to break new ground.

It was well into the process when it received some very interesting news. Located a short distance outside Nevada City, in the same general direction as Ananda, there is a subdivision known as Lake Wildwood. It includes a golf course and some very fine homes. Possibly inspired by the example of Ananda, perhaps independently, Lake Wildwood also filed for municipal incorporation. It too would be a smaller town, but one with enough concrete assets to insure its success as a political entity. While the two petitions are separate, Ananda no longer stands alone. With two petitions before the Nevada County Local Agency Formation Commission more expeditious action is likely to be taken and the two applications are bound, even if indirectly, to reinforce each other.

Forecasting is a hazardous occupation at best, but it is well known that while some of the residents of San Juan Ridge are opposed to Ananda because in their opinion it threatens their life style, the people of the county and of the nearby cities are much more favorable. They are aware that the people of Ananda never create problems such as theft, vandalism or simple bad behavior of any kind. They also are aware that the community is bringing a steady additional cash flow into the area and that the people it attracts as visitors are desirable guests and customers.

Humanity has a well known love affair with the status quo, but it is a losing cause. Changes are inevitable and history reflects the fact that despite everything, society does tend to progress. At one time the issue of slavery was bitterly contested in the United States: today such a confrontation would be unthinkable. Sooner or later, Ananda is almost sure to emerge as the city of Ananda, California.

In his study of Ananda previously cited Nordquist wrote:

> The intent [of the community] is not to undermine or subvert the present society and its institutions, but rather to present an alternative that will reveal the superiority of a life based upon spiritual principles.... The Ananda group, then, cannot be considered as having a belief structure which is 'counter' to the American culture as a whole.

This has now been amply demonstrated. From its unpromising beginning and years of tempering struggle and sacrifice, it has proved its inner strength. The foundation that it has built for itself promises much for its future. And it has already reached out to establish centers in other communities.

More than all of this, it has brought many hundreds of people to a new spiritual awareness; it has, in short, glorified the name of God. And it has done so in a manner that merits both admiration and respect.

Its future will be exciting to behold.